EMPOWERMENT EVALUATION AND SOCIAL JUSTICE

Also from David M. Fetterman

*Collaborative, Participatory, and Empowerment Evaluation:
Stakeholder Involvement Approaches*
David M. Fetterman, Liliana Rodríguez-Campos, Ann P. Zukoski,
and Contributors

Empowerment Evaluation Principles in Practice
Edited by David M. Fetterman and Abraham Wandersman

Empowerment Evaluation and Social Justice

Confronting the Culture of Silence

David M. Fetterman

THE GUILFORD PRESS
New York   London

To Dr. Elsie Fetterman, my 95-year-old mom,
whose heart beats proudly to the rhythm of social justice,
as have her lifelong actions. She will always be known
for her generosity of spirit and enthusiasm for life
and learning. I raise my glass to her—*l'chaim*, to life!

Copyright © 2023 The Guilford Press
A Division of Guilford Publications, Inc.
370 Seventh Avenue, Suite 1200, New York, NY 10001
www.guilford.com

Printed in the United States of America

This book is printed on acid-free paper.

Last digit is print number: 9   8   7   6   5   4   3   2   1

Library of Congress Cataloging-in-Publication Data

Names: Fetterman, David M., author.
Title: Empowerment evaluation and social justice : confronting the culture of
    silence / David M. Fetterman.
Description: New York, NY : The Guilford Press, [2023] | Includes
    bibliographical references and index.
Identifiers: LCCN 2022060234 | ISBN 9781462551958 (paperback) |
    ISBN 9781462551965 (hardcover)
Subjects: LCSH: Social justice. | Evaluation research (Social action
    programs) | Self-actualization (Psychology) | Organizational learning.
Classification: LCC HM671 .F45 2023 | DDC 303.3/72—dc23/eng/20230110
LC record available at *https://lccn.loc.gov/2022060234*

Preface

WHY THIS BOOK IS NEEDED

We face a worldwide crisis at this time in history. COVID, economic instability, global warming, political polarization, gender inequality, racial inequity, LGBTQ+ discrimination, anti-Asian and antisemitic attacks, and an ever-expanding list of critical concerns require our immediate attention. We can't wait for government or industry to save us. We must learn to help ourselves and help others help themselves.

This book is designed to help people become more self-determined, more in control of their own destinies. It provides people with the evaluation tools needed to (1) determine and define their mission or purpose; (2) take stock or assess how well they are doing now; and (3) based on their self-assessment, plan for the future by generating goals, strategies, and credible evidence. This book also provides communities with the tools needed to monitor their progress toward their goals and produce real-world outcomes.

The concerns addressed in this book are not only political, economic, and social in nature; they are also ethical and moral issues. Empowerment evaluation helps people think critically about the world around them. It contributes to learning, illumination, and liberation. Empowerment evaluation is inexorably bound to the pursuit of social justice. It confronts the "culture of silence" that undermines and devalues entire groups of people. Social justice and empowerment evaluation are part of an invisible social contract in our nation and the world. This book attempts to make the invisible visible. It also aims to address issues in the here and now, because justice delayed, including social justice, is justice denied.

AUDIENCE

This book is intended for community activists, community leaders, non-profit directors and staff members, government officials, foundation officers, and industry leaders committed to contributing to their communities, tribal leaders, sovereign nations, evaluators, academics, and anyone concerned with improving the human condition.

It provides a blueprint for action and step-by-step instructions to help build evaluation capacity. Community organizers can use these tools to facilitate change in their communities. Educators can use this book to introduce students to the world of civic responsibility, methodologically sophisticated and sound approaches to contributing to social change and social justice, and conceptual clarity concerning stakeholder involvement approaches to evaluation. Foundation officers, government officials, and industrial philanthropists can use this book to help set change in motion. It provides a detailed portrait of what a healthy and supportive donor relationship looks like with the communities they support.

ORGANIZATION

The book is organized in a manner that allows for multiple uses. The chapters can be read in sequence, particularly for readers who are new to stakeholder involvement approaches or the application of evaluation to social justice concerns. However, for the more seasoned colleague or professional, it allows the reader to zero in on issues of key concern. For example, Chapter 1 presents the definition and scope of empowerment evaluation as well as the connection between empowerment evaluation and Freirean or liberation pedagogy; Chapter 2 explores the theory, concepts, principles (including principles of social justice), and steps of empowerment evaluation; and Chapters 3 and 4 provide real-world social justice-oriented empowerment evaluation case examples, focusing on food justice in the United States and eliminating tuberculosis in India.

Community members, funders, and evaluators can use the tech tools in Chapter 5 to facilitate empowerment evaluations remotely and exponentially expand a community's impact. These tools can be used to reach underserved and often "silenced" populations. Colleagues and community members who are already using empowerment evaluation may only be looking for answers to common questions raised by people immersed in real-world applications. Many of these questions are addressed in Chapter 6, including: "Is empowerment evaluation used for learning or for accountability?" and "Can you use empowerment evaluation to advocate for a program?" Chapter 7 is invaluable for anyone searching for an extensive list of examples of how empowerment evaluation has been used in the fight for social justice. Examples include helping minority youth stay away from tobacco; providing comprehensive sex education to reduce unintended teen pregnancy and HIV/STI rates; raising test scores and increasing student learning in impoverished, formerly segregated rural schools in academic distress; and bridging the digital divide in communities of color. My philosophical position is that one size does not fit all; therefore I have organized the book to respond to multiple and diverse needs.

PEDAGOGICAL FEATURES

I have taught in many countries and for many decades, in the classroom (virtual and face-to-face), in workshops, and in webinars. My mother was also a professor. Teaching is in my blood. If I have learned anything, it is that multiple modalities are needed in order to be effective and help people maximize their potential. In that spirit, I have presented the material in multiple formats, including case examples, sidebars, and glossaries. The case studies apply the concepts and steps in real-life projects and initiatives. They allow the reader to step beyond the theoretical and into the world we live in, attempting to address substantive issues. Sidebars help summarize critical points and crystallize ideas in a few words. Glossaries are needed to help keep track of people, places, and practices in a world of acronyms and complex concepts. In addition, my web page at *drdavidfetterman.com* offers more information and resources pertaining to empowerment evaluation.

ACKNOWLEDGMENTS

First, I would like to express my appreciation to thousands of empowerment evaluators around the world. They have helped me take an idea and place wings on it. Together, we have charted the future of empowerment evaluation by taking calculated risks, applying the approach in real-world settings, constructing a solid theoretical and methodological foundation, producing results, building capacity, and consistently demonstrating our commitment to helping people help themselves.

I am indebted to Lee Cronbach, one of my mentors at Stanford. He generously shared his work with me, including his unpublished manuscripts. He guided me through political and methodological battles. Lee fostered my lifelong commitment to evaluation. I also recognize and value the influence of so many guiding stars in my life, but particularly as a young scholar, Eleanor Chelimsky and Henry Levin.

Abraham Wandersman and I have partnered in the field for over two decades, helping to establish the approach and make it a part of the intellectual landscape. His collegial commitment to quality and his friendship are treasured beyond measure.

I would also like to thank the publishers of the following sources for permission to reprint passages in part or whole:

Fetterman, D. M. (2013). Empowerment evaluation: Learning to think like an evaluator. In M. Alkin (Ed.), *Evaluation roots: A wider perspective of theorists' views and influences* (2nd ed.). Thousand Oaks, CA: Sage.

Fetterman, D. M. (2015). Empowerment evaluation: Theories, principles, concepts, and steps. In D. M. Fetterman, S. Kaftarian, & A. Wandersman (Eds.), *Empowerment evaluation: Knowledge and tools for self-assessment, evaluation capacity building, and accountability* (2nd ed.). Thousand Oaks, CA: Sage.

Fetterman, D. M. (2017). Transformative empowerment evaluation and Freirean pedagogy: Alignment with an emancipatory tradition. *New Directions for Evaluation, 155,* 111–126.

Finally, I am grateful for the valuable feedback I received on various drafts of this book from Tom Summerfelt at Feeding America and Kachina Chawla at USAID. I have had the pleasure and honor of working with C. Deborah Laughton, my editor at The Guilford Press, for over three decades—a consummate editor, close colleague, and good friend. I am also appreciative of the comments and critiques I have received over the decades from Michael Patton, Michael Scriven, Stewart Donaldson, Marvin Alkin, and many others. They have helped enhance my conceptual clarity and refine my methodological sophistication.

Contents

Glossary of Acronyms

ADH—Arkansas Department of Health

AEA—American Evaluation Association

AIDS—acquired immunodeficiency syndrome

ALLIES—Accountability Leadership by Local Communities for Inclusive, Enabling Services

ATLAS.ti—Archiv für Technik, Lebenswelt und Alltagssprache (Archive for Technology, Lifeworld and Everyday Language.text interpretation) (a qualitative data analysis and research software)

BIA—Bureau of Indian Affairs

BIPOC—Black, Indigenous, and people of color

CAF—Community Accountability Framework

CDC—Centers for Disease Control and Prevention

COVID—coronavirus disease (COVID-19); an infectious disease caused by the SARS-CoV-2 virus

CP&E—Collaborative, Participatory, and Empowerment Evaluation Topical Interest Group (division of the AEA)

DHHS—U.S. Department of Health and Human Services

ECB—evaluation capacity building

EFA—Equitable Food Access (Feeding America initiative)

FAQ—frequently asked question

FCC—Federal Communications Commission

GROW—Goal, Reality, Options, and Will coaching model

HyperRESEARCH—qualitative data analysis software

IRB—institutional review board

HP—Hewlett-Packard

LGBTQ+—lesbian, gay, bisexual, transgender, queer (or sometimes questioning), and other sexual orientations and gender identities

MISRGO—Minority Initiative Sub-Recipient Grant Office

NTEP—National Tuberculosis Elimination Programme

NVivo—qualitative data analysis software package (originally NUDIST)

NYC—New York City

REACH—Resource Group for Education and Advocacy for Community Health

SAS—Statistical Analysis System, a statistical software suite

SNAP—Supplemental Nutrition Assistance Program

SPSS—statistical package for social sciences (quantitative data analysis software)

STI—sexually transmitted infections

TB—tuberculosis

TB Champions—tuberculosis survivors who became advocates for people who contracted tuberculosis

UAPB—University of Arkansas at Pine Bluff

UN—United Nations

UNFPA—United Nations Population Fund

URL—Uniform Resource Locator (a web address)

USAID—United States Agency for International Development

USDA—U.S. Department of Agriculture

USDE—U.S. Department of Education

WHO—World Health Organization

WIC—Women, Infants, and Children Supplemental Nutrition Program

Introduction

The sounds of the culture of silence can be deafening but must be heard.

Empowerment evaluation is grounded in an emancipatory tradition. It is designed to help people learn to confront the status quo by questioning assumptions and prescribed roles, unpacking myths, rejecting dehumanization, and no longer blindly accepting the "truth" about how things are or can be. Empowerment evaluation helps people think critically about the world around them.

Empowerment evaluation is also inexorably bound to the pursuit of social justice. Social justice is fundamentally about fairness. It involves respecting and protecting everyone's human rights. Social justice applies to a wide variety of areas, including health care, education, employment, housing, and safety. It requires access to essentials; being heard (and not silenced), including hearing marginalized and vulnerable voices; participation; and equity. A few of the most pressing social justice issues include racial equity, gender equality, and LGBTQ+ rights. See Figure 1.1.

The interwoven threads of social justice and empowerment evaluation are visible in each chapter of this book. For example, in this chapter, the relationship between empowerment evaluation and Freirean pedagogy is explored.

Freirean pedagogy is a teaching philosophy that invites educators to encourage students to question the status quo, critique existing power structures, and assert their rights. It is a philosophy of liberation in which people are responsible for taking charge of their own lives and leading the effort to liberate themselves. It is the opposite of traditional pedagogies that are often referred to as the "banking model of education," which

FIGURE 1.1. Equality, equity, and liberation. *Source:* Interaction Institute for Social Change. Artist: Angus Maguire.

views students as empty vessels to be filled with facts and knowledge. Freirean pedagogy views the learner as a co-creator of knowledge.

Chapter 1 highlights how empowerment evaluation contributes to learning, illumination, and liberation. It also discusses how empowerment evaluation attacks the "culture of silence" that undermines and devalues entire groups of people. Chapter 2 focuses on the essentials of empowerment evaluation and highlights how social justice is one of empowerment evaluation's principles. It makes the case that evaluation can and should be used to address social inequalities in society. The case examples in Chapters 3 and 4 focus on social justice issues: food justice and eliminating tuberculosis. Chapter 5 demonstrates how to use tech tools to invite participation, help silenced voices to be heard, and exponentially expand a community's impact. Chapter 6 responds to questions ranging from "Is empowerment evaluation used for learning or accountability?" to "Can you use empowerment evaluation to advocate for a program?" Chapter 7 concludes the book with a clear commitment to social justice and highlights concrete case examples. They include tobacco prevention and cessation initiatives, schools in academic distress, sex education programs, bridging the digital divide in communities of color, tuberculosis elimination, and fighting for food justice. Social justice and empowerment evaluation are part of an invisible social contract in our nation and the world, and this book attempts to make the invisible visible.

The purpose of empowerment evaluation is empowerment. It aims to cultivate and enhance self-determination and self-efficacy. Empowerment evaluation helps people help themselves by taking more control over their lives and improving their life trajectories. Empowerment evaluation is typically an ongoing or formative stakeholder involvement approach, where people take responsibility for monitoring and evaluating their progress, with a focus on results, outcomes, and impact. It can also be summative in nature, helping a group make go–no-go decisions concerning the continuation or elimination of specific programs or initiatives.

> Empowerment evaluation helps people help themselves.

DEFINITION

Empowerment evaluation is the use of evaluation concepts, techniques, and findings to foster improvement and self-determination (Fetterman, 1994). It is an approach that "aims to increase the likelihood that programs will achieve results by increasing the capacity of program stakeholders to plan, implement, and evaluate their own programs" (Wandersman et al., 2005, p. 28). It is the "Give a person a fish, and you feed them for a day. Teach a person to fish, and you feed them for a lifetime" concept applied to evaluation. It cultivates a sense of ownership and is mainstreamed as part of the planning and management of a program or organization. In essence, empowerment evaluation is a tool to help people produce desired outcomes and reach their goals.

> "Give a person a fish, and you feed them for a day. Teach a person to fish, and you feed them for a lifetime."

SCOPE

Empowerment evaluation has become a global phenomenon, reaching the four corners of the earth in less than a couple of decades. It is operating in over 18 countries, including Australia, Brazil, Canada, Ethiopia, Finland, India, Israel, Japan, Mexico, New Zealand, South Africa, South Korea, Spain, Thailand, the United Kingdom, and the United States. It is a change process that has supported people and communities in improving their lives in places ranging from small townships in South Africa where sustainable community health initiatives were created to large-scale Silicon Valley corporations, including Hewlett-Packard and Google, where the process helped to build tech and small-business capacity in communities of color.

Empowerment evaluation has been used by the Office of Special Education and Rehabilitation Services of the U.S. Department of Education (USDOE) to foster self-determination. Likewise it has branched out to many additional areas, including schools in academic distress (Fetterman, 2005b), accreditation in higher education (Fetterman, 2012), minority tobacco-use prevention (Fetterman, Delaney, Triana-Tremain, & Evans-Lee, 2015), and medical education (Fetterman, 2009a; Fetterman, Deitz, & Gesundheit, 2010). It has been used by Peruvian women artisans to build sustainable businesses (Sastre-Merino, Vidueira, Díaz-Puente, & Fernández-Moral, 2015), by teachers to evaluate their own performance (Clinton & Hattie, 2015), and by fourth and fifth graders to enhance diversity and inclusion (Langhout & Fernandez, 2015). Empowerment evaluation has been applied to night ministries as well as rabbinical colleges. It can be found operating in child abuse prevention programs as well as in after-school program collaborations.

Hewlett-Packard's (HP) $15 million Digital Village initiative received national and international attention in 2001. It was designed to bridge the digital divide in communities of color. The Tribal Digital Village, one of the HP Digital Villages composed of 18 Native American tribes, used empowerment evaluation to guide its self-reflection and assessment, inform decision making, and construct strategic plans. It helped the Digital Village build technological and economic infrastructures on their reservations (Fetterman, 2013a). Specifically, the Tribal Digital Village used empowerment evaluation to build one of the largest unlicensed wireless systems in the country as well as operate a digital printing press (as an alternative to gaming). The former head of the Federal Communications Commission (FCC) praised their efforts. The media also showered empowerment evaluation with accolades given its role in support of this social justice initiative (*www.drdavidfetterman.com/general-5-12*).

Stanford University School of Medicine's empowerment evaluation represents another well-recognized contribution to educational transformation. Stanford's curriculum was rooted in a traditional Flexnerian model, which called for 2 years of science and then 2 years of clinical work. However, medical students typically want to work with patients right away. There is no logical reason to delay the process of having medical students work with patients, in some cases if only to learn they are not a good match for the profession. Empowerment evaluation was used to help inform curricular decision making, transforming Stanford's curriculum into a more clinical mode from day one (Fetterman et al.,

2010). In addition, there were unintentional redundancies and a less-than-optimal curricular progression that needed attention. The process was placed in the hands of faculty, students, staff members, and administrators in order to help them participate in the systemic changes. Patients were also involved in the courses to enhance the clinical dimension.

Course and clerkship ratings were one measure of student satisfaction with the curricular transformation. In comparing evaluation results before and after the stakeholders began using this approach (and in essence took control of their own evaluation), we found that the average student ratings for required courses improved significantly ($p = .04$; student's one-sample t test). The approach also helped students prepare and pass accreditation review (with flying colors). In essence, empowerment evaluation provided all participants with a mechanism to cultivate ownership, guide curricular decision making and reform, and produce desired outcomes. Their use of empowerment evaluation helped set a higher standard for medical schools throughout the country.

Empowerment evaluation has also been used to facilitate evaluations remotely in BIPOC (Black, Indigenous, and people of color) communities, including addiction studies programs (Fetterman, 2022) and tobacco-prevention initiatives (Fetterman, Delaney, et al., 2015). The Feeding America empowerment evaluation work, presented in Chapter 3, highlights the social justice dimension of this stakeholder involvement approach. Feeding America is using empowerment evaluation to help food banks across the United States combat food insecurity and establish food security and food justice from a racial equity perspective. Similarly, a United States Agency for International Development (USAID)-funded empowerment evaluation effort to eliminate tuberculosis in India is explored and unpacked in Chapter 4, highlighting principles of social justice, inclusion, capacity building, and accountability.

Empowerment evaluation is not limited by type of program. In addition to the long list of programs mentioned earlier, it has even been used in reaching for the stars, contributing to the NASA/Jet Propulsion Laboratory's efforts to educate youth about the prototype Mars rover (Fetterman & Bowman, 2002).

EMPOWERMENT EVALUATION AND FREIREAN PEDAGOGY

Empowerment evaluation contributes to learning, illumination, and liberation, as much as to accountability. It has a synergistic relationship with Freirean pedagogy (Freire, 1974, 1985). They are both forms of transformative education. They create environments conducive to people empowering themselves. They rely on cycles of reflection and action to contribute to transformation. They both attack the "culture of silence" (acquiescence to a pervasive system of beliefs that undermine and devalue entire groups of people). Empowerment evaluation and Freirean pedagogy share a common belief that:

> "Every person, however . . . submerged in the 'culture of silence,' can look critically at his or her world through a process of dialogue with others" (Shaull, 1974, p. 13).

> Every person, however . . . submerged in the "culture of silence," can look critically at his or her world through a process of dialogue with others, and can gradually come to perceive his personal and social reality, think about it, and take action in regard to it. (Shaull, 1974, p. 13)

This stands in juxtaposition to educational approaches that are designed to reproduce the status quo. As Shaull (1974) explains:

> There is no such thing as a neutral educational process. Education either functions as an instrument which is used to facilitate integration of the younger generation into the logic of the present system and bring about conformity or it becomes the practice of freedom, the means by which men and women deal critically and creatively with reality and discover how to participate in the transformation of their world. (p. 15)

Empowerment evaluation and Freirean pedagogy are both dedicated to the concepts of community and collaboration, as well as to self-determination, social justice, and sustainability. Empowerment evaluation and Freirean pedagogy are aligned in principle and practice.

TWO STREAMS

Empowerment evaluation in practice is typically applied along two streams. The first is practical and the second transformative. Practical empowerment evaluation is similar to formative evaluation. It is designed to enhance program performance and productivity. It is still controlled by program staff, participants, and community members. However, the focus is on practical problem solving, as well as on programmatic improvements and outcomes.

Transformative empowerment evaluation (Fetterman, 2015a) highlights the psychological, social, and political power of liberation. People learn how to take greater control of their own lives and the resources around them. The focus in transformative empowerment evaluation is on liberation from predetermined, conventional roles and organizational structures or "ways of doing things." In addition, empowerment is a more explicit and apparent goal. Freirean pedagogy is most closely aligned with transformative empowerment evaluation in that it is committed to helping people confront the culture of silence about the status quo and raise consciousness about their role in the world (as compared with "false consciousness"[1]).

HISTORICAL HIGHLIGHTS

A brief glimpse into the major phases of empowerment evaluation's development demonstrates how (with some evaluation community soul searching, missteps, detours, and resistance) the approach ultimately triumphed, compelling all of us to "walk our talk." It also highlights an empowerment evaluator's receptiveness to critique and dialogue. The result of decades of discourse is enhanced conceptual clarity and methodological specificity.

Empowerment Evaluation's Introduction to the Field: Einstein and Arrow

The roots of empowerment evaluation influenced its practice (see Christie & Alkin, 2013; Alkin & Christie, 2004). Empowerment evaluation was introduced in a presidential address at the American Evaluation Association (AEA; Fetterman, 1994). The empowerment evaluation approach was painted with broad strokes focusing on its definition, conceptual roots, and facets—including facilitation, advocacy, illumination, and liberation.

Albert Einstein, an actor, helped me introduce the approach. I taught him about evaluation and empowerment evaluation in preparation for

---

[1] The culture of silence is designed to indoctrinate and condition people to think of themselves as useless, without value, and incapable of making a meaningful contribution to society.

his presentation. People thought he was brilliant. His evaluation presentation or performance was sprinkled with Einstein aphorisms like:

- "We cannot solve our problems with the same thinking we used when we created them."
- "No problem can be solved from the same level of consciousness that created it."
- "Logic will get you from A to B. Imagination will take you everywhere."
- "The whole of science is nothing more than a refinement of everyday thinking."
- "Anyone who has never made a mistake has never tried anything new."
- "The only source of knowledge is experience."

These quotations were in alignment with empowerment evaluation principles and practices. They spoke to the need to take a leap of faith and trust in people's innate cognitive abilities to solve their own problems, grounded in their own experience.

A second plenary speaker helped to introduce the approach. He was Kenneth Arrow, a Nobel laureate from Stanford University. We had spoken about empowerment evaluation while I was developing it. Encouraged by what he heard, he jumped at the chance to share his comments about this burgeoning approach to evaluation. He spoke eloquently about the increasing importance of evaluation in society and the significance of empowerment evaluation in our global sphere. His credentials added to the credibility and legitimacy of the endeavor, but empowerment evaluation's credibility ultimately rested on hard-headed arguments and examples.

Our presentations stimulated conversations and arguments that spilled out into the hallways during the conference. We were asking colleagues fundamental questions. We were asking them to question everything they had been taught and long since taken for granted. What is evaluation? What was the purpose of evaluation? Who is in charge? Who are we as evaluators?

It was a heady time. The attention, the excitement, and the wonder were palpable. The new approach created a tremendous amount of intellectual and emotional excitement and commentary. It was an idea "whose time had come." The approach was embraced by evaluators from around the world. The possibilities seemed endless. We had no idea what the magnitude of the impact of this new approach would be in the field and in the world. The ripples were almost instantly felt worldwide, in large part owing to the development of the Internet (Fetterman, 2001b). We had tapped into a need to actualize underutilized human potential.

Empowerment Evaluation in Turmoil: The Debates

Where else but in this extended family of evaluators can you expect both an attack and an embrace in the same breath? The AEA is a place where evaluators can be vulnerable, open ourselves up for critique, and learn from the experience. The magnitude of the upheaval that followed, however, was unanticipated. The empowerment evaluation approach was met with excitement, applause, and hope. However, it was also met with disdain and fear (and more than a little microaggression). It made many evaluators rethink what evaluation was and what it meant to be an evaluator. Basically, it put the association and our colleagues to the test. Were we giving evaluation away or building evaluation capacity to help people conduct their own evaluations? Were we the external experts or coaches and critical friends?

Introducing empowerment evaluation to the field touched a nerve among many traditional evaluators, resulting in highly charged exchanges in *Evaluation Practice* (Fetterman, 1995; Stufflebeam, 1994). Stufflebeam (1994), Scriven (1997), and Sechrest (1997), for example, called empowerment evaluation a "movement" because of the rapid pace and global scope of adoption. Stufflebeam was worried that empowerment evaluation might violate the standards (as if there was only one right way to conduct an evaluation). He also thought it was not objective and explicitly stated it was "not where we should go in the future."

Some of the arguments in the journals reached a feverish pitch. A few were so pointed and personal that one of the editors, Blaine Worthen (1997), had to assert civility standards and take a stand against ad hominem remarks.

The empowerment evaluation camp responded to each of the issues raised, typically in a point–counterpoint manner in the journals. We also were aware of the larger implicit issues at play. We explicitly raised the issue of positions of privilege.

Empowerment evaluation is grounded in my work with the most marginalized and disenfranchised population, ranging from urban school systems to community health programs in South African townships. They have educated me about what is possible in communities overwhelmed by violence, poverty, disease, and neglect. They have also repeatedly sensitized me to the power of positions of privilege. One dominant group has the vision, makes and changes the rules, enforces the standards, and need never question its own position or seriously consider any other. In such a view, differences become deficits, rather than additive elements of culture. People in positions of privilege dismiss the contributions of a multicultural world. They create rational policies and procedures that systematically deny full participation in their community to people who think and behave differently.

Evaluators cannot afford to be unreflective about the culturally embedded nature of our profession. There are many tacit prejudgments and omissions embedded in our primarily Western thought and behavior. These values, often assumed to be superior, are considered natural. However, Western philosophies have privileged their own traditions and used them to judge others who may not share them, disparaging such factors as ethnicity and gender. In addition, they systematically exclude other ways of knowing. (Fetterman, 1995, p. 190)

Wild's comments (1997, p. 172), in a book review, captured the tone of the times when empowerment evaluation was first introduced. "This is a significant addition to the library of evaluation, and the writers should be congratulated for bringing together such a solid collection. Fetterman et al. have nailed their theses to the door of the cathedral. Now the question is, how tolerant is the establishment of dissent?"

> "Fetterman et al. have nailed their theses to the door of the cathedral. Now the question is, how tolerant is the establishment of dissent?" (Wild, 1997).

Empowerment Evaluation: A Time to Collect Our Thoughts

The more common critiques were sincere and sought to understand the concept, seeking greater clarity. Our exchange, in the same evaluation journals, allowed us to collect our thoughts, respond to misconceptions, learn from our antagonists, and commit what we were learning to paper (and to digital formats as well).

The introduction of empowerment evaluation to the AEA and the resulting dialogues led to the first collection of literature about this approach, beginning with *Empowerment Evaluation: Knowledge and Tools for Self-Assessment and Accountability* (Fetterman, Kaftarian, & Wandersman, 1996). The book highlighted the work of the W. K. Kellogg Foundation, a well-recognized philanthropic organization, and the Accelerated Schools Project, a national educational reform movement, both of which adopted empowerment evaluation. Demonstrating the breadth and depth of empowerment evaluation, this book presented case examples that ranged from battered women's shelters to HIV-prevention initiatives. In launching a new approach to evaluation, the book also represented a fundamental developmental stage in empowerment evaluation.

A second book, *Foundations of Empowerment Evaluation* (Fetterman, 2001a), raised the bar in empowerment evaluation. While it respected other approaches, the book provided a clear three-step approach to empowerment evaluation. In utilizing case examples, including a high-stakes higher education accreditation self-study, the book also applied particular standards to empowerment evaluation, including utility, feasibility, propriety, and accuracy standards (see Joint Committee on Standards for Educational Evaluation, 1994). *Foundations of Empowerment Evaluation* made several additional contributions, including:

1. Explaining the role of process use (as people conduct their own evaluations).
2. Comparing collaborative, participatory, and empowerment evaluation.
3. Discussing similarities with utilization-focused evaluation.
4. Discussing the multiple purposes of evaluation, including program development, accountability, and knowledge.

This collection was followed by a number of articles and contributions to encyclopedic and leading texts in the field (e.g., Fetterman, 2004a, 2004b; Wandersman et al., 2004). Empowerment evaluation, at that stage of development, had become a part of the intellectual landscape of evaluation (Fetterman, 2004a, 2005a).

Empowerment Evaluation Principles in Practice (Fetterman & Wandersman, 2005) represented a milestone in the development of empowerment evaluation. In pursuit of additional conceptual clarity, it elaborated on the existing definitions of empowerment evaluation, emphasizing capacity building, outcomes, and institutionalization. In addition, the book made explicit the 10 principles guiding the approach. The principles are as follows:

1. Improvement
2. Community ownership
3. Inclusion
4. Democratic participation
5. Social justice
6. Community knowledge
7. Evidence-based strategies
8. Capacity building
9. Organizational learning
10. Accountability

These principles were developed to guide empowerment evaluation from conceptualization to implementation and served as a lens through which to focus an evaluation.

Empowerment Evaluation in the Digital Villages: Hewlett-Packard's $15 Million Race Toward Social Justice (Fetterman, 2013a) represented a quantum leap in the empowerment evaluation and social justice space in targeting a technologically sophisticated social justice issue: bridging the digital divide in communities of color. The story documented the implementation of a large-scale, multisite, ethnically diverse, comprehensive community initiative and its corresponding empowerment evaluation. The project was high profile from the beginning; its launch included a former president of the United States, HP's Chief Executive Officer, and a human rights activist. The book thrust the project into the national spotlight.

The Digital Villages comprised 18 Native American tribes and lower socioeconomic Black, Latinx, and Pacific Islander neighborhoods. Each community had explicit goals, specific strategies, and agreed-upon evidence to document its progress and outcomes.

Empowerment evaluation became internalized and institutionalized as part of the project's planning and operations. In the process, it too was thrust into the limelight. Successes and missteps became larger than life. The successes ranged from building the largest unlicensed wireless system in the country to exponentially expanding employment and skills training centers. Less than optimal performances included the inability to coalesce and create partnerships and allowing site participants to uninvite the host to a site visit when they needed to be encouraged to trust the funder and ask for assistance. We all could have served as better mirrors for that site.

Overall, however, the Digital Villages was a success story. Significant goals and enhanced economic opportunity in disenfranchised American communities were accomplished. The Digital Villages became a part of civil rights and social justice history in America. The project was also an opportunity to demonstrate how evaluation can contribute to the pursuit of social justice.

The second edition of *Empowerment Evaluation: Knowledge and Tools for Self-Assessment, Evaluation Capacity Building and Accountability* (Fetterman, Kaftarian, & Wandersman, 2015) began as a "simple" revision of *Empowerment Evaluation: Knowledge and Tools for Self-Assessment and Accountability* (Fetterman et al., 1996), the book that helped launch the empowerment evaluation approach. However, in the process of creating a "simple" updated revision, every single chapter was replaced. In addition, principles and tools that did not exist when the approach was first launched were added. The revision was so radical that even the title of the book was changed to explicitly include the term *evaluation capacity building*. Nevertheless, the book highlighted the theory, principles, concepts, and steps of empowerment evaluation. Case examples included Peruvian women using the approach to improve their craft-making skills and market their crafts online, teachers using empowerment evaluation to improve their teaching and learning methods, Native Americans using the method to bridge the digital divide in communities of color, fourth- and fifth-grade students using the approach to make their school become more welcoming, and community health care activists implementing tobacco-prevention projects designed to keep minority youth away from tobacco. This collection of case histories represented a transformative leap that was literally decades beyond the first endeavor.

The response was enthusiastic and overwhelmingly positive. Loisellin Datta, a luminary in the field of evaluation, who was one of the first to review the book, concluded: "Read this 2015 edition, particularly for readers new to evaluation who want, in one place, a compendium of what empowerment evaluation is about, a statement of its principles, a set of case examples in diverse settings, and an understanding of where Fetterman, Kaftarian, and Wandersman are *now* in their thinking" (2016, p. 3). She also commented on the maturation of the arguments and exchanges that contributed to the collection: "Each critique was responded to by Fetterman, not a man to be intimidated, in a dialogue that over the decades seems marked by growing mutual understanding, preciseness, and respect. . . . Thus, the context of the 2015 edition is the continuation of clarification, refinements, and examples, even if the conversation has now moved far from hallway near riots toward appreciative acceptance" (2016, p. 2).

Stewart Donaldson summed up the overarching sentiment about the book and the approach in the Foreword: "One of the greatest evaluation innovations of the past two decades has been the development of a professional and systematic approach to self-evaluation called empowerment evaluation" (2015, p. x).

Collaborative, Participatory, and Empowerment Evaluation: Stakeholder Involvement Approaches (Fetterman, Rodríguez-Campos, Zukoski, & Contributors, 2018) helped place empowerment evaluation in the context of a stakeholder involvement approach to evaluation. The book identified the essential features of each of these stakeholder approaches to evaluation, defining and differentiating among them. It has helped evaluators select the most appropriate approach for the task at hand, and has also served to educate funders and community members as they select the most appropriate approach for them. The book provides an overview of each approach, including a definition, essential features, conceptual framework, advantages, the role of the evaluator, guiding principles, and the steps associated with applying each approach. Each approach is followed by two case examples.

> "One of the greatest evaluation innovations of the past two decades has been the development of a professional and systematic approach to self-evaluation called empowerment evaluation" (Donaldson, 2015, p. x).

The empowerment evaluation examples include an evaluation in Google, a corporate tech giant, and a nonprofit organization that managed a comprehensive sex education initiative. Colleagues from the AEA's Collaborative, Participatory, and Empowerment Evaluation Topical Interest Group had been calling for a book defining the differences between stakeholder involvement approaches in actual practice for over a decade. This collection further contributed to conceptual clarity. Once again, Lois-ellin Datta (2018) reviewed the contributions in this book and summed up her laudatory comments in the following passage:

> This valuable book both shows and tells on the hot topic of collaborative, participatory, and empowerment approaches. Each "essentials" chapter gains impact from two chapters illustrating what the principles look like in actual evaluation practice. Beautifully explanatory, memorably demonstrated! The authors emphasize understanding in order to select the most

appropriate stakeholder approaches for the situation at hand. Far from claiming the exclusive benefits of any single approach, the book is infused with the spirit of working together. The chapter on commonalities powerfully lays out the features of stakeholder involvement at macro-, mid-, and microlevels of analysis, creating a strong theory-to-practice bridge for newcomers as well as experts. I wish I could gift-wrap this book and send it express to evaluation practitioners in fields from agronomy to zoology.

In addition to all of these books on empowerment evaluation, classic debates with Michael Scriven, Michael Patton, Marvin Alkin, and Stewart Donaldson, to mention only a few, exemplified the honest and simultaneously critical dialogue required for us to grow, evolve, and transform (Donaldson, Patton, Fetterman, & Scriven, 2010; Patton, 1997a, 2015; Scriven, 1997).

Empowerment Evaluation: Institutionalized

Our "21st-birthday party" panel at the AEA represented the culmination of decades of dialogue (Fetterman & Wandersman, 2017). Donaldson (2017; see also 2015) commented that empowerment evaluation was "an approach that has literally altered the landscape of evaluation." Michael Patton (2017) explained what was "exemplary is its openness to dialogue, reflective practice and process use." Michael Scriven (2017) stated, "There is much to admire about empowerment evaluation." Their earlier critiques (often razor sharp) helped us enhance our conceptual clarity and methodological specificity. As Edmund Burke (in *Reflections on the Revolution in France*, 1790), said, "He [or she] that wrestles with us strengthens our nerves and sharpens our skills. Our antagonist is our helper."

Today, six books later, empowerment evaluation is now practiced worldwide. Our projects focus on health, education, and the general welfare of communities. We address social justice issues ranging from food security/insecurity (and food justice) to the elimination of tuberculosis throughout India.

> "He [or she] that wrestles with us strengthens our nerves and sharpens our skills. Our antagonist is our helper" (Burke, 1790).

Numerous empowerment evaluators have been recognized and received awards for their use of empowerment evaluation, including Abraham Wandersman (2008 Outstanding Publication Award), Margret Dugan (1995 Guttentag Award for a promising scholar), Shakeh

Kaftarian (1996 Myrdal Award for Evaluation Practice), and myself (1995 Myrdal Award for Evaluation Practice; 2000 Lazarsfeld Evaluation Theory Award). Another indicator of its institutionalization is the existence of the Collaborative, Participatory and Empowerment Evaluation Topic Interest Group division of the AEA. Liliana Rodríguez-Campos and I are co-chairs of this stakeholder involvement approach to evaluation division.

Empowerment evaluation is a part of the intellectual landscape in evaluation, in large part because it works. In addition, it has been integrated into the field because our colleagues were able to rise to the occasion and (with some detours, bumps, and bruises) apply core evaluation values to our efforts to improve the human condition.

Essential Features

Theories, Concepts, Principles, and Steps

When you know what you are talking about,
you have the essentials.

The essence of empowerment evaluation is a systematic way of thinking. Empowerment evaluation is a constellation of theories, principles, concepts, and steps that are used to guide practice. Empowerment evaluation is more than the sum of its parts, including its "essential" parts. It is the gestalt or whole package that makes it work. Together empowerment evaluation ideas, values, and practices help people learn how to think like an evaluator. People develop their evaluation capacity in the process of evaluating the impact of their own work. This approach to evaluation fosters improvement and self-determination.

Empowerment evaluation theories, principles, concepts, and steps are interrelated and reinforcing. The theories provide a 30,000-foot view of the approach, while the steps provide a turn-by-turn set of instructions. Together they provide a rich and layered map of the dynamic terrain of empowerment evaluation.

The theories guiding empowerment evaluation, as noted earlier, include empowerment and self-determination theories, as well as specific evaluation theories, including process use and theories of use and action. In turn, these theories help inform the 10 overarching principles that provide empowerment evaluation with an explicit direction and purpose, beginning with improvement and continuing to accountability. The key concepts that help define empowerment evaluation include critical friends, cultures of evidence, cycles of reflection and action, communities of learners, and reflective practitioners.

They are sequentially ordered conceptual building blocks. Once defined, they begin with the macro or highest level of abstraction, consisting of the guiding theories, and end at the micro level, consisting of the specific steps of empowerment evaluation. The sequence is designed to help practitioners understand and implement empowerment evaluation practice. These conceptual building blocks are briefly discussed in the following sections. A detailed description is provided in *Empowerment Evaluation: Knowledge and Tools for Self-Assessment, Evaluation Capacity Building, and Accountability* (Fetterman, Kaftarian, et al., 2015).

THEORIES

An exploration into the theories guiding empowerment practice helps to illuminate the integral relationship between method and use in empowerment evaluation. The most pertinent theories guiding empowerment evaluation are empowerment theory, self-determination theory, process use theory, and theories of use and action. *Empowerment theory* is divided into processes and outcomes. This theory has implications for the role of the empowerment evaluator or facilitator, which differs from a traditional evaluator. *Self-determination* is one of the foundational concepts underlying empowerment theory, and it helps to detail the specific mechanisms or behaviors that enable the actualization of empowerment. *Process use* represents much of the rationale or logic underlying empowerment evaluation in practice because it cultivates ownership by placing the approach in community and staff members' hands. Finally, the alignment of *theories of use and action* explains how empowerment evaluation helps people produce desired results.

Empowerment Theory

Empowerment theory is about gaining control, obtaining resources, and understanding one's social environment. It is also about problem solving, leadership, and decision making. Empowerment processes are empowering if they help people develop skills so that they can become independent problem solvers and decision makers (Zimmerman, 2000).

Empowerment theory processes contribute to specific outcomes. Linking the processes to outcomes helps outline a chain of reasoning. When specified outcomes are achieved, it is possible to retrace the steps taken to determine which processes were most effective. Similarly, when specific processes are implemented poorly, the contributing factors associated with a failure to achieve specified outcomes are easier to see.

Empowerment theory focuses on the positive rather than on the negative. For example, the language of empowerment focuses on wellness as compared with illness, competence compared with deficits, and strength compared with weakness (Perkins & Zimmerman, 1995). Moreover, empowerment theory highlights capabilities instead of risk factors and environmental influences instead of views that blame the victim (Fetterman, 1981). Empowerment theory is in accord with the Freirean tradition, in that people are required to take an active role in their own transformation and take action to gain greater control over their lives. Empowerment evaluation and Freirean pedagogy provide people with the conceptual skills that are required to critically understand their social environment and become independent problem solvers (Fetterman, 2017).

Self-Determination

Self-determination is one of the foundational concepts underlying empowerment theory and is defined as the ability to chart one's own course in life. The concept of self-determination details specific mechanisms that help program staff members and participants implement an empowerment evaluation.

It consists of numerous interconnected capabilities, such as the ability to identify and express needs; establish goals or expectations and a plan of action to achieve them; identify resources; make rational choices from among various alternative courses of action; take appropriate steps to pursue objectives; evaluate short- and long-term results, including reassessing plans and expectations and taking necessary detours; and persist in the pursuit of those goals. They are the instrumental microsteps required for people to accomplish their objectives, build confidence, design new challenging goals, and ultimately take charge of their own lives. Freire recognized the need for people to take action grounded in reality to transform their lives. These steps are a blueprint for action on a microlevel.

Process Use

Process use represents much of the rationale or logic underlying empowerment evaluation in practice because it cultivates ownership by placing the approach in community and staff members' hands. Community and program members pose the evaluation questions (within the context of their preestablished commitments to funders and community members). They collect and analyze the data, make meaning from the data, and report learnings (with the assistance of a critical friend or empowerment evaluator).

The more that people are engaged in conducting their own evaluations, the more likely they are to believe in them, because the evaluation findings are their own. In addition, a by-product of this experience is that they learn to think evaluatively. When they do so, they are more likely to make decisions and take actions based on their evaluation data. This way of thinking is at the heart of process use (see Patton, 1997b, 2005).

> The more that people are engaged in conducting their own evaluations, the more likely they are to believe in them, because the evaluation findings are their own.

In an empowerment evaluation, thinking evaluatively is a product of guided immersion. Guided immersion occurs when people conduct their own evaluation (immersed in the experience), assisted (or guided) by an empowerment evaluator. Teaching people to think evaluatively is like teaching them to fish, as noted earlier. It can last a lifetime and is what evaluative sustainability is all about—internalizing evaluation.

Empowerment evaluation models a Freirean liberating pedagogy in part because it recognizes the importance of people, instead of outside experts, remaining in control of their own lives. As Freire (1974) warned, "The fact that investigators may in the first stage of the investigation approximately apprehend the complex of contradictions does not authorize them to begin to structure the program content of educational action. This perception of reality is still their own not that of the people" (p. 106).

Empowerment evaluation assumes that people learn and internalize that learning from doing. Freire (1974) observed that it is only when people "become involved in the organized struggle for their liberation that they begin to believe in themselves" (p. 52). Moreover, people learn, become more fully conscious, and are liberated by conducting their own evaluations. Freire (1974) captured this self-reflective phenomenon when he explained that people's oppression itself needs to be the basis for reflection, which leads to the type and level of engagement required for liberation.

This pedagogy makes oppression and its causes objects of reflection by the oppressed, and from that reflection will come their necessary engagement in the struggle for their liberation. And in the struggle this pedagogy will be made and remade. (p. 33)

Bias is another concern that is raised about people engaged in evaluating themselves. It assumes that people will be self-congratulatory or at least not objective. However, Freire (1974) points out the flaw in that thinking:

Some may think it inadvisable to include the people as investigators in the search for their own meaningful thematics: that their intrusive influence will "adulterate" the findings and thereby sacrifice the objectivity of the investigation. This view mistakenly presupposes that themes exist, in their original objective purity, outside men [and women]—as if these were things. Actually, themes exist in men [and women] in their relations with the world, with reference to concrete facts. . . . There is, therefore, a relation between the given objective fact, the perception men [and women] have of this fact, and the generative themes. (pp. 97–98)

No pedagogy is truly liberating if it continues to treat people as "unfortunates" and offers models from those in power. People "must be their own example in the struggle" (p. 39). This is how conscientização (or conscientization— "the process by which human beings participate critically in a transforming act"; Freire, 1985, p. 106) is achieved and people become free "to create and construct, to wonder, and to venture" (Freire, 1985, p. 55). (See also Fetterman & Wandersman, 2007, for a response to the role of bias.)

> People's oppression itself needs to be the basis for reflection, which leads to the type and level of engagement required for liberation.

Empowerment evaluation invites, if not demands, participation. Participation or immersion is a form of experiential education. Guided, this immersion helps people to see the world through an evaluative lens. Participation also creates an authentic, credible, and almost palpable sense of ownership. The ownership created through this level of stakeholder involvement in turn enhances credibility, follow-through, and sustainability. People find it credible because they create, conduct, and own the evaluation. It is this combination of evaluative thought and ownership, through immersion, that makes empowerment evaluation work, improving knowledge utilization in the process.

Theories of Use and Action

Once the groundwork is laid with the empowerment, self-determination, and process use theories, conceptual mechanisms become more meaningful. Theories that enable comparisons between use and action are essential. The approach works best when the pieces are in place. When things go wrong, which is normal in life, it is possible to identify and compare the areas needing attention.

Empowerment evaluation relies on the reciprocal relationship between theories of use and action at every step in the process. A *theory of action* is usually the espoused operating theory about how a program or organization works. It is a useful tool, generally based on the views of program personnel. This theory of action is often compared with the theory of use. The theory of use is the actual program reality, or the observable behavior of stakeholders (see Argyris & Schon, 1978; Patton, 1997b). People engaged in empowerment evaluations create a theory of action at one stage and test it against the existing theory of use during a later stage. Similarly, they create a new theory of action as they plan for the future. Because empowerment evaluation is an ongoing and iterative process, stakeholders test their theories of action against their theories of use during various microcycles to determine whether their strategies are being implemented as recommended or designed. The theories go hand in hand in empowerment evaluation.

These theories are used to identify gross differences between the ideal and the real. Communities of empowerment evaluation practice compare their theory of action with their theory of use in an effort to reduce the gap between them. This is the conceptual space where most communities of empowerment evaluation practice strive to accomplish their goals as they close the gap between the theories (see Fetterman, 2013b).

The process of empowerment embraces the tension between the two types of theories and offers a means for reconciling incongruities. The dialectic in which theories of action and use are routinely juxtaposed helps community and staff members test the degree of alignment between what their organization or community espouses and what it does in practice. In the process, in daily practice, it creates a culture of learning and evaluation. More to the point it forces communities and organizations to "walk their talk" and

> The dialectic between theories of action and use helps community and staff members test the degree of alignment between what their community espouses and does in practice.

more closely approximate what they espouse. Once again, it helps people think like evaluators.

Freire recommended dialogue and discussion, followed by action, and then reflection on practice again. In essence, he suggested a comparison of precisely these theories. The juxtaposition of theories of use and action are the mechanisms by which people improve upon their capacity to learn, and as Freire suggested, to adapt to the world, intervene, recreate, and transform it.

PRINCIPLES

Empowerment evaluation is guided by 10 specific principles (Fetterman & Wandersman, 2005, pp. 1–2, 27–41, 42–72; Fetterman, 2015c, pp. 27–28). They work synergistically, providing a sense of direction and purposefulness throughout an evaluation. They include:

1. Improvement—designed to help people improve program performance and to help them build on their successes and reevaluate areas meriting attention.

2. Community ownership—values and facilitates community control; use and sustainability are dependent on a sense of ownership.

3. Inclusion—invites involvement, participation, and diversity; contributions come from all social and economic levels and all walks of life.

4. Democratic participation—participation and decision making should be open and fair.

5. Social justice—evaluation can and should be used to address social inequities in society.

6. Community knowledge—respects and values the knowledge of community members.

7. Evidence-based strategies—respects and uses the knowledge base of scholars (in conjunction with community knowledge).

8. Capacity building—designed to enhance stakeholders' ability to conduct evaluations and to improve program planning and implementation.

9. Organizational learning—data should be used to evaluate new practices, inform decision making, and implement program practices; used to help organizations learn from their experience (building on successes, learning from mistakes, and making midcourse corrections).

10. Accountability—focused on outcomes and accountability; functions within the context of existing policies, standards, and measures of accountability; did the program accomplish its objectives?

Empowerment evaluation principles help evaluators and community members make decisions that are in alignment with the larger purpose or goals associated with capacity building and self-determination. For example, the aim of the improvement principle is to help people improve their programs and practice and succeed in accomplishing their objectives. Community ownership is required to make this happen in a meaningful and sustained manner. Authentic community ownership requires inclusion. A single elite group cannot make all the decisions. People from all parts of an organization and/or community should be involved. The principles of inclusion remind evaluators and community members to include, rather than exclude, members of the community, even though fiscal, logistic, and personality factors might suggest otherwise. The capacity-building principle reminds the evaluator to provide community members with the opportunity to collect their own data, even though it might initially be faster and easier for the evaluator to collect the same information. Capacity building contributes to the production of outcomes (see Labin, Duffy, Meyers, Wandersman, & Lesesne, 2013). The community ownership principle fosters self-determination and responsibility, instead of dependency, by putting evaluation in the hands of program staff and participants.

> The capacity-building principle reminds the evaluator to provide community members with the opportunity to collect their own data, even though it might initially be faster and easier for the evaluator to collect the same information.

The accountability principle guides community members to hold one another accountable. It also situates the evaluation within the context of external requirements and credible results or outcomes. (See Fetterman, 2005a, p. 2.)

Empowerment evaluators, funders, staff, and community members share a common commitment to producing results. The list of real-word outcomes associated with empowerment evaluations is both long and significant (see Fetterman, Kaftarian, et al., 2015).

The interconnected, interrelated, and reinforcing nature of empowerment evaluation gives it strength and sustainability. The same type of synergy and interconnectivity applies to the remaining combination of principles (see Fetterman & Wandersman, 2005, pp. 210–212, for details). However, empowerment evaluation is not a one-size-fits-all approach. It is designed to help people conscientiously assess the impact of their work, which is shaped by and needs to be adapted to local circumstances, conditions, and needs.

Participation from many stakeholders is critical if the effort is to be credible and taken seriously. It is also more efficient to include major stakeholders at the beginning of a project rather than having to revisit each of the issues every time a new group of people is invited to participate.

These principles are in alignment with Freirean pedagogy. For example, the principles of community ownership, inclusion, and democratic decision making highlight the significance of community involvement and control. Community members are expected to authentically participate in, if not control, evaluation-related decision making concerning issues that directly affect their lives. Empowerment evaluation and Freirean pedagogy agree that the presence of people struggling "for their liberation will be what it should be: not pseudo-participation, but committed involvement" (Freire, 1974, p. 56). In addition, empowerment evaluation's commitment to social justice shares the same Freirean assumptions about the world, specifically that there are inequities throughout the world and there is a pressing need to address them in a timely manner—through action. Accountability, for both empowerment evaluation and Freirean discourse, is paramount. It must be preceded by dialogue and understanding, but it is one of the best tests of effectiveness. Accountability, in this case, refers to both individual responsibility to the group and the group's responsibility to larger societal forces, including producing outcomes. Although each principle is important, the community is in the best position to highlight the principles that best match its needs. The emphasis is dependent on community context and capacity.

Many of these principles are aspirational and inspirational. They help us visualize what is possible and what we should strive for in our lives. In reality, we only approximate these principles at best, but that should not discourage or divert us from striving for the lofty ideals represented by these guiding principles.

CONCEPTS AND ROLES

Empowerment evaluation concepts provide a more instrumental view of how to implement the approach. Key concepts include critical friends, cultures of evidence, cycles of reflection and action, communities of learners, and reflective practitioners. A critical friend is an evaluator who facilitates the process and steps of empowerment evaluation. This person believes in the purpose of the program, but provides constructive feedback, and helps to ensure that the evaluation remains organized, rigorous, and honest.

Critical Friends

Relationships play a pivotal role in the process of conducting an empowerment evaluation. The role of the critical friend merits attention because it is like a fulcrum in terms of fundamental relationships. Applied improperly, the role can be like a wedge inhibiting movement and change; applied correctly, it can be used to leverage and maximize the potential of a group.

Zimmerman's (2000) characterization of the community psychologist's role in empowerment activities is easily adapted to the empowerment evaluator. It also demonstrates the impact of theory on practice, shaping every dimension of the approach, including the evaluator's role.

> An empowerment approach to intervention design, implementation, and evaluation redefines the professional's role relationship with the target population. The professional's role becomes one of collaborator and facilitator rather than expert and counselor. As collaborators, professionals learn about the participants through their cultures, their worldviews, and their life struggles. The professional works *with* participants instead of advocating *for* them. The professional's skills, interest, or plans are not imposed on the community; rather, professionals become a resource for a community. This role relationship suggests that what professionals do will depend on the particular place and people with whom they are working, rather than on the technologies that are predetermined to be applied in all situations.

Empowerment evaluators have considerable expertise, but as critical friends or coaches they help keep the evaluation systematic, rigorous, and on track. They are able to function in this capacity by advising, rather than directing or controlling, an evaluation. They provide a structure or set of steps for conducting an evaluation. They recommend, rather than require, specific activities and tools. They listen and rely on the group members' knowledge and understanding of their local situation.

Some people ask how can empowerment evaluators be objective and critical if they are friends and favor a specific type of program. The answer is simple: empowerment evaluators are critical and objective because they want the program to work (or to work better). They may favor a general type of program but do not take a position about it before they have the data to make an informed choice.

The empowerment evaluator differs from many traditional evaluators. Instead of being the "expert" who is completely independent, separate, and detached from the people he or she works with, so as not to get "contaminated" or "biased," the empowerment evaluator works closely with and alongside program staff members and participants.

This approach is aligned with Freirean pedagogy, in which the leader works closely with the community, not as an outside expert who is distant from the community. In both approaches, the evaluator or facilitator refrains from assuming control, framing the discussion, dominating the dialogue, or prescribing action plans. Instead, the group takes the lead and works together as a group. Freire (1974) draws a similar picture of the role in his comparison of teachers and students:

> Teachers and students [leadership and people], co-intent on reality are both Subjects, not only in the task of unveiling that reality and thereby coming to know it critically, but in the task of re-creating that knowledge. As they attain this knowledge of reality through common reflection and action, they discover themselves as its permanent re-creators. (p. 56)

The Freirean facilitator and empowerment evaluator both serve the group or community in an attempt to help them maximize their potential and unleash their creative and productive energy for a common good. Important attributes of a critical friend include creating an environment conductive to dialogue and discussion; providing or requesting data to inform decision making; facilitating rather than leading; and being open to ideas, inclusive, and willing to learn (see Fetterman, 2009a; Fetterman et al., 2010, for additional details about this role).

> The Freirean facilitator and empowerment evaluator both serve the community to help them maximize their potential and unleash their creative and productive energy for a common good.

Empowerment evaluators help cultivate a culture of evidence by asking people why they believe what they believe. People are asked for evidence or documentation at every stage so that it becomes normal and expected to have data to support one's opinions and views. Empowerment evaluators are essential because they help ground the group in data and data-driven decision making.

Capacity Building

Capacity building has been a driving force in empowerment evaluation since its inception (Fetterman, 1994; Fetterman, Kaftarian, et al., 1996). The evaluation capacity literature has coincided and intersected with the empowerment evaluation. (For more information about evaluation capacity building, see Duffy & Wandersman, 2007; Taylor-Ritzler, Suarez-Balcazar, Garcia-Iriarte, Henry, & Balcazar, 2013.)

Labin et al. (2013) define *evaluation capacity building* (ECB) as "an intentional process to increase individual motivation, knowledge, and skills, and to enhance a group or organization's ability to conduct or use evaluation" (p. 2). The assumption is that ECB strategies will improve individual attitudes, knowledge, and skills as evidenced by behavioral changes. In addition, ECB strategies will facilitate sustainable organizational learning.

Freire (1985) also believed in the capacity of ordinary citizens (literate or illiterate) to analyze their own reality, to "'re-consider' through the 'considerations' of others, their own previous 'consideration.'" The purpose of "individuals analyzing their own reality is to become aware of their prior, distorted perceptions, and thereby to have a new perception of that reality" (p. 114). Empowerment evaluation and Freirean practice use many of the same mechanisms or procedures to build a reflective, sustainable evaluative capacity and culture—placing the work in the hands of the people themselves (with guidance).

Cycles of Reflection and Action

Empowerment evaluation involves ongoing phases of analysis, decision making, and implementation (based on evaluation findings). The process is a cyclical process. Programs are dynamic, not static, and require continual feedback as they change and evolve. Freire (1974) described the same process in the context of transformation (p. 36) and liberation, explaining that "reflection—true reflection—leads to action. On the other hand, when the situation calls for action, that action will constitute an authentic praxis only if its consequences become the object of critical reflection" (pp. 52–53).

Cycles of reflection and action are ongoing processes that contribute to long-term, sustainable forms of social change and transformation. It is in this cyclical testing of ideas and strategies in practice (and revision based on feedback) in the real world that knowledge is gained. As Freire (1974) explains: "Knowledge emerges only through invention and re-invention, through the restless, impatient, continuing, hopeful inquiry human beings pursue in the world, with the world, and with each other" (p. 58). Cycles of reflection and action are successful when they are institutionalized and become a normal part of the planning and management of the program.

Communities of Learners

Empowerment evaluation is driven by a group process. It creates a community of learners. Members of the group learn from each other, serving as their own peer review group, critical friends, resources, and norming mechanisms. Individual members of the group hold each other accountable concerning progress toward stated goals.

> Empowerment evaluation is driven by a group process. It creates a community of learners.

Freire (1974) was also committed to group learning and believed that real change could not be accomplished by the individual alone but needed to be understood and accomplished through the group (pp. 34, 52, 88, 100). As Freire explained:

> I can not think for others or without others, nor can others think for me. Even if the people's thinking is superstitious or naive, it is only as they rethink their assumptions in action that they can change. Producing and acting upon their own ideas—not consuming those of others. (p. 100)

Reflective Practitioners

Finally, empowerment evaluations and Freirean pedagogy help create reflective practitioners. Reflective practitioners use data to inform their decisions and actions concerning their own daily activities. This practice produces self-aware and self-actualized individuals who have the capacity to apply this worldview to all aspects of their lives. As individuals develop and enhance their own capacity, they improve the quality of the group's exchanges, deliberations, and action plans.

A LIFT UP

Empowerment evaluation and Freire's liberating educational approach help raise consciousness and encourage people to take responsibility for their own lives. They help people engage in cycles of reflection and action in order to become more critically aware of their existence, to take steps to improve their performance as members of a group, and to contribute to their community's development. These approaches help lift people up, instead of pushing them down (see also Lentz et al., 2005).

STEPS

There are many ways in which to conduct an empowerment evaluation. The three-step approach provides people with a logic model that, like a highway, they build while driving on it. Their Plans for the Future or intervention is rooted in a self-assessment (or Taking Stock exercise), and the self-assessment is rooted in their Mission. This approach creates a common thread or chain of reasoning. In addition, focusing on the Mission, or "big picture," refining the group's efforts by prioritizing the most important activities to monitor and evaluate as a group, and then implementing Plans for the Future (based on Taking Stock assessments and exchange) produces a greater "dose effect"—refocusing the group's efforts from a large-scale, big-picture Mission to a small list of critical activities.

> The three-step approach provides people with a logic model that, like a highway, they build while driving on it.

Adopting and applying a three-step (or an alternative 10-step) approach makes it easy to certify that an empowerment evaluation approach is being adopted (within the context of the theories, concepts, and principles presented). However, they are not the only steps used to facilitate an empowerment evaluation. Stories, maps of the "journey," and other graphics have been used effectively. The specific steps selected to facilitate an empowerment evaluation are only limited by our creativity and imagination. However, the selected steps should model the logic and values associated with these two popular and effective approaches if they are to conform with some meaningful fidelity to the model.

There are many ways in which to implement an empowerment evaluation. In fact, empowerment evaluation has accumulated a warehouse of useful tools. The three-step approach to empowerment evaluation is one of the most popular tools in the collection (Fetterman, 2001). It includes helping a group (1) establish its Mission, (2) Take Stock of its current status, and (3) Plan for the Future. The popularity of this particular approach is in part a result of its simplicity, effectiveness, and transparency.

Mission

The group comes to a consensus concerning its Mission, or values. This gives the members a shared vision of what's important to them and where they want to go. The empowerment evaluator facilitates this process by asking participants to generate statements that reflect their Mission. These phrases are recorded on a poster sheet of paper (and may be projected on an LCD projector depending on the technology available). Alternatively, participants can collaborate remotely with the use of various online programs (discussed in Chapter 5). These phrases are used to draft a Mission statement (crafted by a member of the group and the empowerment evaluator). The draft is circulated among the members. They are asked to "approve" it and/or suggest specific changes in wording as needed. A consensus about the Mission statement (see Figure 2.1)

Mission

preparation for the 21st century
universal access to health, literacy,
and education
social justice

FIGURE 2.1. Mission.

helps the group think clearly about their self-assessment and Plans for the Future. It anchors the group in common values.

Taking Stock (Part I: Prioritization)

After coming to a consensus about the Mission, the group evaluates its efforts (within the context of a set of shared values). First, the empowerment evaluator helps members of the group generate a list of the most important activities required to accomplish organizational or programmatic goals. The empowerment evaluator gives each participant five dot stickers, and asks the participants to place them by the activities they think are the most important to accomplish their programmatic and organizational goals (and thus the most important to evaluate as a group from that point on). They can put one sticker on five different activities or all five on one activity if they are concerned that the activity will not get enough votes (see Figure 2.2). Once again, this entire process can be adapted for remote work and conducted online as needed. The top 10 items with the most dots represent the results of the prioritization part of Taking Stock. The 10 activities represent the heart of Part II of Taking Stock: rating and dialogue.

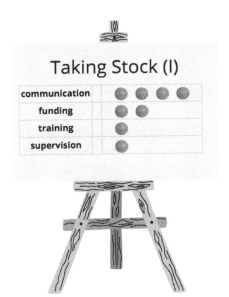

FIGURE 2.2. Taking Stock: Part I (Prioritization).

Taking Stock (Part II: Rating and Dialogue)

The empowerment evaluator asks participants in the group to rate how well they are conducting each of the selected activities, using a scale of 1 (low) to 10 (high). The columns are averaged horizontally and vertically (see Figure 2.3). Vertically, the group can see who is typically optimistic and/or pessimistic. This helps the group calibrate or evaluate the ratings and opinions of each individual member and helps the group establish norms. Horizontally, the averages provide the group with a consolidated view of how well (or poorly) the work is going. The empowerment evaluator facilitates a discussion and dialogue about the ratings, asking participants why they rated a certain activity a 3 or a 7.

Dialogue

The dialogue about the ratings is one of the most important parts of the process. In addition to clarifying issues, evidence is used to support viewpoints, and "sacred cows" are surfaced and examined.

> The dialogue about the ratings is one of the most important parts of the process.

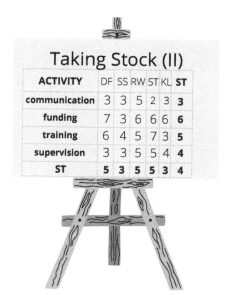

Taking Stock (II)

ACTIVITY	DF	SS	RW	ST	KL	**ST**
communication	3	3	5	2	3	**3**
funding	7	3	6	6	6	**6**
training	6	4	5	7	3	**5**
supervision	3	3	5	5	4	**4**
ST	**5**	**3**	**5**	**5**	**3**	**4**

FIGURE 2.3. Taking Stock: Part II (Rating and Dialogue).

Generative Themes

The process of engaging in empowerment evaluation generates priorities for inquiry that are similar to what Freire (1974) referred to as "generative themes." Without these generative themes, critical topics and issues may never be made explicit and thus never grappled with. Freire (1974) observed that these

> themes may or may not be perceived in their true significance. They may simply be felt—sometimes not even that. But the nonexistence of themes within the sub-units is absolutely impossible. The fact that individuals in a certain area do not perceive a generative theme, or perceive it in a distorted way, may only reveal a limit-situation . . . in which men (and women) are still submerged. (p. 94)

Generative themes provide the relevant substance for active engagement—the issues that people are most concerned about. This sets the stage for one of the most important parts of the process—authentic dialogue. Similar to Freirean pedagogy, through dialogue, existing thoughts will change and new knowledge will be created.

Moreover, the process of specifying the reason or evidence for a priority provides the group with a more efficient and focused manner of identifying what needs to be done next, during the Planning for the Future step of the process. Instead of generating an unwieldy list of strategies and solutions that may or may not be relevant to the issues at hand, the group can focus its energies on the specific concerns and reasons for a low performance rating that were raised in the dialogue or exchange.

The dialogue is analytical and often emotional. Empowerment evaluation has responded to critiques focused on an objectivist perspective without sufficient attention to emotion (Fetterman, 1995, 2001; Stufflebeam, 1994). Freire (1974) recognized the dialectical nature of these human features. On the one hand, Freire highlighted the value of "objectively verifiable" (p. 35) data. However, he also observed: "One cannot conceive of objectivity without subjectivity" (p. 35). The subjective and the objective are in a "constant dialectical relationship" (p. 35). Freire (1997) referred to this as "reason soaked with emotion" (p. 165).

Empowerment evaluation embraces this combination. People have emotions. Emotions are a powerful force shaping people's consciousness and action. According to Freire (1974), "To deny the importance of subjectivity in the process of transforming the world and history is naïve and simplistic" (p. 35).

A mere perception of reality not followed by this critical intervention (objectifying and acting upon that reality) will not lead to a transformation of objective reality—precisely because it is not a true perception. This is the case of a purely subjectivist perception by someone who forsakes objective reality and creates a false substitute. (Freire, 1974, p. 37)

Dialogue is a critical part of the pedagogy of critical consciousness or conscientização. People confront each other with an evaluative view of the functionality, productivity, and adaptability of their community and where it is situated in the larger society. They create meaning by sharing their view of reality with each other and coming to a consensus about the world they live in and what needs to be done next to improve their lives.

> "To deny the importance of subjectivity in the process of transforming the world and history is naïve and simplistic" (Freire, 1974, p. 35).

This is often where the "elephant" in the room emerges, or the underlying problem or inequity that everyone knows about, but no one is willing to surface and discuss in daily life. The dialogue moves the group beyond needs to causes that link to their perceived needs. Logic models and theories of change (without the jargon or terminology) become more meaningful and useful. Critical dialogue contributes to critical consciousness. Reflection based on a critical dialogue propels groups into action. According to Freire (1974) "critical dialogue presupposes action" (p. 167). Planning for the Future, in empowerment evaluation, is built on the critical dialogue or Taking Stock exchanges. It represents the co-constructed road map (or intervention) required to accomplish community goals.

Planning for the Future

Many evaluations conclude at the Taking Stock phase. However, Taking Stock is a baseline and a launching-off point for the rest of the evaluation. After rating and discussing programmatic activities, it is important to do something about the findings. It is time to Plan for the Future (see Figure 2.4). This step involves generating goals, strategies, and credible evidence, (to determine if the strategies are being implemented and if they are effective). The goals are directly related to the activities selected in the Taking Stock steps. For example, if communication was selected,

> Taking Stock activities guide Planning for the Future goals, and Taking Stock evidence guides Planning for the Future strategies.

FIGURE 2.4. Planning for the Future.

rated, and discussed, then communication (or improving communication) should be one of the goals. The strategies emerge from the Taking Stock discussion as well, as noted earlier. For example, if communication received a low rating and one of the reasons was because the group never had agendas for its meetings, then preparing agendas might become a recommended strategy in the Planning for the Future exercise.

Planning for the Future can only be conducted after the group has Taken Stock of its situation. In other words, their plan of action, similar to Freirean steps, follows the dialogue (Taking Stock). In addition, Taking Stock is preceded by an initial discussion about the group's purpose or Mission. This discussion provides an intellectual coherence to the endeavor and, as in the Freirean pedagogy, provides an internal theory guiding practice and action. However, raising consciousness, implementing action plans, and testing hypotheses require monitoring if the initiatives are to produce the desired outcomes (and remain on track and timely).

MONITORING (EVALUATION DASHBOARD)

The evaluation dashboard helps build capacity by providing people with a tool they create to help them monitor their own performance over time. The dashboard is shared with the evaluation team, administrators, and sponsors. The dashboard is used to signal the need for help, support, and guidance, not shame, blame, or stigmatiza-

tion. It also helps community members learn how to determine when it is necessary to make midcourse corrections. Ultimately, this tool is designed to help people stay on track concern-ing their desired goals and bring support when needed (before it is too late). This positive,

> The evaluation dashboard is designed to help people stay on track concerning their desired goals and bring support when needed (before it is too late).

nurturing, and constructive approach is essential to a healthy and pro-ductive form of empowerment evaluation.

Many programs, projects, and evaluations fail at this stage for lack of individual and group accountability. Individuals who spoke eloquently and/or emotionally about a certain topic should be asked to volunteer to lead specific task forces to respond to identified problems or concerns. They do not have to complete the task. However, they are responsible for taking the lead in a circumscribed area (a specific goal) and reporting the status of the effort periodically at ongoing management meetings. Simi-larly, the group should make a commitment to reviewing the status of these new strategies as a group (and be willing to make midcourse corrections if they are not working). Conventional and innovative evaluation tools are used to monitor the strategies; these tools include online surveys, focus groups, and interviews, as well as the use of a quasi-experimental design (if appropriate). In addition, program-specific metrics are developed using baselines, milestones, and goals (as deemed useful and appropriate). For example, a minority tobacco-prevention program empowerment evalua-tion in Arkansas has established the following metrics:

1. Baselines (the number of smoke-free parks in their county)
2. Goals (the number of smoke-free parks they plan to establish by the end of the year)
3. Milestones (the number of smoke-free parks they plan to estab-lish each quarter)
4. Actual performance (the number of smoke-free parks they estab-lish)

The actual performance is compared with the milestones and goals in order to determine if the group is making progress (see Figure 2.5). These metrics are used to help a community monitor program-implementation efforts and enable program staff and community mem-

Number of Smoke-Free Parks

QTR	1st Qtr	2nd Qtr	3rd Qtr	4th Qtr
Actual Performance	3	8	15	20
Milestones	5	10	15	20
Goals	20	20	20	20
Baseline	1	1	1	1

FIGURE 2.5. Comparing quarterly milestones and goals with actual performance.

bers to make midcourse corrections and replace ineffective strategies with potentially more effective ones as needed. The metrics are not used to chastise, stigmatize, or ostracize individuals. They simply serve to signal when the group needs assistance. These data are also invaluable when group members conduct a second Taking Stock exercise (3 to 6 months later) to determine if they are making progress toward their desired goals and objectives.

> The metrics are not used to chastise, stigmatize, or ostracize individuals. They simply serve to signal when the group needs assistance.

This approach is aligned with Freirean pedagogy because it places the tools to monitor performance in the hands of the people in the community. It is transparent, enabling staff and community members to monitor their own performance, while allowing sponsors to determine if additional assistance is needed along the way. It is also a tool to build evaluation capacity because it teaches people how to monitor their own performance and learn to make adjustments in a timely fashion.

CONCLUSION

The journey from theory to practice and back again in empowerment evaluation has been long and often difficult, but productive. We appreciate how far we have come, and that our approach is placed in the "pantheon of major approaches" (Patton, 2015, p. 15) and is viewed as "one of the greatest evaluation innovations of the past two decades" by Donaldson (2015, p. ix). Nevertheless, we recognize how much more work lies ahead as we continue to enhance conceptual clarity and methodological specificity. We live in a world where, without warning, the entire planet and our continued existence as a species is called into question by global warming, social inequities, nuclear threats, and even a microscopic virus. These challenges only strengthen our resolve to continue to learn how to adapt this global phenomenon to a world that is, in theory, in a constant state of change.

Empowerment evaluation and Freirean pedagogy are aligned in both theory and practice. The alignment is most pronounced with transformative empowerment evaluation. However, both streams of empowerment evaluation embrace essential features, including critical thinking, authentic dialogue, *conscientização*, and action. Empowerment evaluation and Freirean pedagogy are emancipatory and, if applied appropriately, help people free themselves from the constraints placed on them as well as the limitations they place on themselves. Together, they can also help to transform the practice of evaluation.

3

Integrating Empowerment Evaluation within a Preexisting Evaluation and Recognizing Donors as Change Agents

Feeding America's Fight for Food Justice in the United States

Nature abhors a vacuum; empowerment is no different.

Empowerment evaluations have been successful as the primary evaluation framework in settings throughout the world as discussed earlier, ranging from townships in South Africa to Google in Silicon Valley. The outcomes and impacts have been significant: bridging the digital divide in communities of color, transforming schools from academic distress to success, and preventing and stopping minority youth from using tobacco, to name a few (Fetterman, 2001, 2013a, 2018; Fetterman, Kaftarian, et al., 2015; Fetterman et al., 2018; Fetterman & Wandersman, 2005). However, one of the most common questions raised in empowerment evaluation webinars and workshops is: Can an empowerment evaluation be conducted when there is a preexisting evaluation framework and specific requirements?

Empowerment evaluations are not conducted in a vacuum.

The answer is yes. Empowerment evaluations are not conducted in a vacuum. They are conducted within the context of what the group is already being held accountable to complete or produce.

The problem is that very few communities are given the opportunity to map out their plans to produce outcomes. Communities lack a sense of ownership when it comes to external evaluation questions and frameworks, which makes them less credible and less sustainable.

Communities and program staff members accept external evaluations as part of the "devils bargain," a requirement of the funding. However, they do not welcome a series of irrelevant questions to respond to or to impose on their clients, partners, or neighbors. These evaluation questions are often viewed as a distraction from or a drain on direct program services.

Nevertheless, external evaluation frameworks and questions can be reframed and become invaluable. The integration of empowerment evaluation into an existing system typically requires two steps backward before moving forward with a meaningful and sustainable effort.

BACKTRACKING TO MAKE PREEXISTING FRAMEWORKS MEANINGFUL

First, the group must be given the opportunity to assess its performance within the context of the existing contractual arrangements. The assessment begins by conducting the Mission and the Taking Stock steps of the process.

Second, after group members complete the Taking Stock exercise and launch their Planning for the Future step, they need tools to determine if their strategies are being implemented and if they are effective. At this point, preexisting surveys, interview protocols, and scheduled observations become invaluable. There are already-made (and required) data collection activities that can be used to answer the group's questions about whether their strategies are being applied and if they are effective.

Backtracking and giving community members the opportunity to reestablish their Mission, Take Stock of their efforts, and Plan for the Future can make the preexisting evaluation frameworks meaningful and even useful. This approach helps community members take control of the inquiry and simultaneously embrace the preexisting survey questions (because now they address the questions they've asked themselves, instead of responding to a series of external, perfunctory, and often disruptive lines of inquiry).

> Empowerment evaluation helps community members take control of the inquiry and simultaneously embrace the preexisting survey questions (because now they address the questions they've asked themselves, instead of responding to a series of external, perfunctory, and often disruptive lines of inquiry).

An abbreviated Feeding America empowerment-evaluation exercise with a focus on racial equity is presented in this chapter. It demonstrates how empowerment evaluation and the preexisting surveys were integrated and made meaningful to the community of grantees.

PROGRAM AND INITIATIVE DESCRIPTION

More than 38 million people, including 12 million children, experience food insecurity in the United States (United States Department of Agriculture [Coleman-Jensen, Rabbitt, Gregory, & Singh, 2021]). Feeding America is a nationwide network of over 200 food banks serving over 46 million people. The organization has ambitious goals. According to Claire Babineaux-Fontenot, CEO of Feeding America, "Feeding America has a bold aspiration that every community and each person within it has access to the food and resources that they say they desire and need to thrive."

> More than 38 million people, including 12 million children, experience food insecurity in the United States (USDA; Coleman-Jensen, Rabbitt, Gregory, & Singh, 2021).

On September 28, 2022, the Biden Administration held the first White House Conference on Hunger, Nutrition, and Health in over 50 years. The CEO committed to a date on the goal: "We are excited to partner with the White House on this conference to help achieve the goal of ending hunger by 2030."

Within this context, Feeding America facilitated a Starbucks-funded initiative to encourage 15 food banks to apply a racial equity lens to their work. An empowerment evaluation approach was used to help them establish their goals, monitor individual and group food bank progress, and assess their performance. The emphasis was on learning. However, the evaluation also contributed to accountability by providing food bank grantees with the tools they needed to enhance the probability of reaching their goals.

STEPS TO INTEGRATE EMPOWERMENT EVALUATION AND PREEXISTING SURVEYS

The first step toward making the preexisting survey questions meaningful involved reviewing the contractual agreement and the questions. The questions had been vetted and looked appropriate on the surface.

The intent was to save the grantees time and energy by providing them with a long list of preexisting questions. However, the sheer number of survey questions for grantees to consider was overwhelming. Navigating through the large bank of survey questions to find the right ones was like conducting a search in the dark in a methodological blizzard without a flashlight. The absence of a clear focus and plan concerning survey question selection also raised concerns about the potential for a significant respondent burden.

The next step involved discussing the less than optimal (but understandable) grantee reaction to being asked to use the survey questions. They did not appear to be useful, and the grantees did not want to subject their clients or neighbors to these surveys. Administering the survey was viewed as a logistical nightmare by some of the grantees. Fundamentally, however, the grantees did not own the survey questions. They could not see the value added in asking people to answer them, and they were viewed as both time-consuming and potentially disruptive to their operations. In essence, there was no place for these questions (and this task) in their implicit theory of change or logic model. The survey was not part of their logical chain of reasoning.

The third step required (1) a hard stop, (2) an admission of error—sharing that a mistake was made by not consulting the grantees first, (3) acknowledging that we were all learning together and that we didn't have all the answers, and (4) stating that it was time to try a new approach that placed control of the evaluation back in the hands of the grantees.

CONDUCTING THE THREE STEPS

We restarted the inquiry by conducting a three-step empowerment evaluation series of exercises. The food banks as a group stated their overall Mission. They brainstormed and generated a long list of the most important activities they engaged in to accomplish their Mission. Then they prioritized the list, selecting the top 10 activities (those that received the most votes).

The grantees rated how well they were conducting the top 10 activities using a scale of 1 (low) to 10 (high). The dialogue about the ratings was illuminating, often surfacing the "elephant in the room." One of the elephants in the room was how we were defining food insecurity and food justice. This dialogue led to an exploration into how we defined food sovereignty as well.

Building on the Taking Stock step, the grantees developed a Plan for the Future. The goals were based on the activities that were rated and discussed. Similarly, the strategies were drawn from the evidence provided during the Taking Stock exchange.

Then the group was in a position to meaningfully examine the utility of the required survey questions. Many of the preexisting questions were suddenly relevant and could be used to collect the data required to determine if their Plans for the Future were working. There was no reason to reinvent the wheel. The same questions that grantees initially objected to when delivered out of context were embraced because the answers to them would provide necessary information. The exercise resulted in meeting contractual obligations by reframing the same survey questions within the grantees' contextual framework, understandings, and needs.

> The dialogue about the ratings was illuminating, often surfacing the "elephant in the room." One of the elephants in the room was how were we defining food insecurity and food justice. This dialogue led to an exploration into how we defined food sovereignty as well.

FEEDING AMERICA AND FOOD JUSTICE: A CASE EXAMPLE

The first step involved facilitating a discussion or dialogue about the Mission or purpose of Feeding America's (Starbucks-funded) Equitable Food Access initiative. The group's comments concerning the Mission ranged from cultivating trusting relationships to creating sustainable feedback loops with communities to improve distribution services. An abbreviated list of grantee Mission statements is provided below.

Mission Statements

- Equitable access to nutritious foods
- Nutrition education in the community
- Providing immediate access to nutritious foods
- Erasing/diminishing disparities in accessing nutritious food
- Better communication with the agencies and the neighbors we collectively serve
- Education on food insecurity!

- Center the experiences and voices of partners and community members in the process
- Improve upon our methods of impact related to the social impact of food insecurity
- Increase access to and distribution of healthy foods in our most rural and underserved communities
- Continuous learning on how to be more strategic and collaborative in what data we collect, how we collect and use the data, and how we can share the data to aid in data-driven decision making
- Building trusting relationships between the community in need and the providers of services
- Support local economies in purchasing local products
- Address disparities in food and beyond-food access
- Building a framework to help food banks practice more equitable distribution to BIPOC and rural communities
- Develop sustainable and impactful partnerships between corporate sponsors and food banks and the communities they serve
- Create pathways of service for individuals and/or families in need so there is "no wrong door" for families to engage in service and resources
- Measure the impact of new corporate nonprofit partnerships to gauge success and replicability
- Engage and listen to the community prior to making strategic decisions
- Create sustainable feedback loops to connect with communities to continue to improve distribution services

Equitable Food Access colleagues then drafted a preliminary summary of their Mission for future use.

Taking Stock I (Brainstorming and Prioritization)

Equitable Food Access colleagues shifted gears and transitioned from focusing on their Mission to Taking Stock of their current efforts. They brainstormed a list of key activities that contributed to their Mission. Then they were given five "votes" to determine the most important activities to rate and evaluate as a group from that point on. The activities receiving the most "votes" are listed as follows:

- Identify partners who can amplify and broaden your engagement.
- Understand the intersection of race and food insecurity in each community.
- Identify demographic groups in high need and their geography.
- Seek and gather feedback from communities we serve to identify inclusive best practices.
- Develop data gathering and analysis tools to track progress and understand impact, bringing more voices to the table for added insight in decision-making practices.
- Identify access barriers and determine solutions.
- Provide critical data and findings to support decision making to create a greater impact.
- Develop resource lists for both culturally relevant foods, procurement processes, and beyond-food (SNAP, WIC, etc.) engagement opportunities.
- Improve operations and systems to better serve those in need.
- Provide client-choice distributions (enabling people to pick the amount and types of food they want rather than prebagging and boxing food).
- Gather community input.
- Create and disseminate accessible collateral materials (flyers, brochures, social media, outreach, etc.).

An illustration of their prioritization effort, using Google Sheets, is presented in Figures 3.1 and 3.2.

Taking Stock II (Rating and Dialogue)

Equitable Food Access group members rated these activities on a scale of 1 (low) to 10 (high). I facilitated a discussion about the ratings by asking members of the group to share their reasons and evidence for their ratings. This exercise helped the group identify patterns or themes in common, as well as divergent assessments of program effectiveness. The evidence provided during the discussion by each member was

> The evidence provided during the discussion by each member was used to guide the development of the strategies proposed in the Plans for the Future step.

used to guide the development of the strategies proposed in the Planning for the Future step. An abbreviated version of the group's ratings is presented in Figures 3.3 and 3.4.

In addition to asking participants their reason for their ratings, I also asked them what it would take for them to assign higher ratings for each activity. This question prompted them to outline the steps they believed were needed to improve program outcomes and impact. For example, concerning the activity "Identify demographic groups in high need and their geography," one participant said, "We do a good job of identifying groups in high need, but we could do even better if we spoke directly with the clients."

> I also asked participants what it would take for them to assign higher ratings for each activity. This prompted them to outline the steps they believed were needed to improve program outcomes and impact.

FIGURE 3.1. Prioritization. "Voting" for the most important activities to rate, discuss, and evaluate. The total votes are given in the left column, and individual votes are given in the right columns.

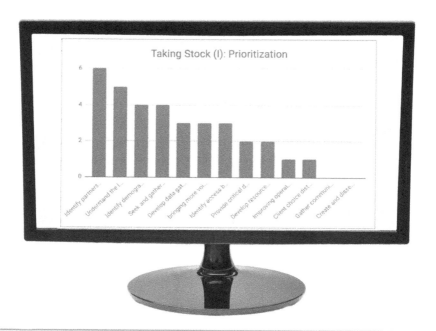

FIGURE 3.2. Prioritization graph. Graphically highlighting the results of the prioritization exercise.

AVG		ZH	CC	EW	CSM	WK
5.60	Identify partners who can amplify and broaden your engagement	4	6	4	7	7
5.60	Understand the intersection of race and food insecurity in each community	6	6	5	6	5
6.20	Identify demographic groups in high need and their geography	5	7	5	8	6
3.60	Seek and gather feedback from communities we serve to identify inclusive best practices	3	4	2	4	5
		4.5	5.75	4	6.25	5.75

FIGURE 3.3. Ratings. Average ratings are in the left-hand column. Individual ratings, using a scale of 1 (low) to 10 (high), are in the right-hand columns.

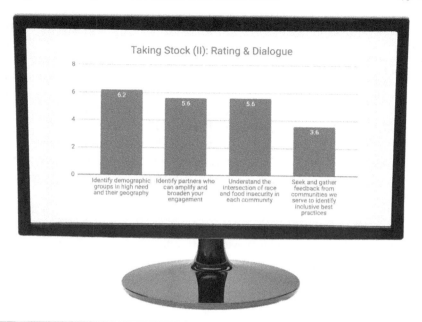

FIGURE 3.4. Ratings graph. Graphically highlighting the results of the ratings exercise.

Similarly, concerning the activity "Identify partners who can amplify and broaden your engagement," a few suggestions included more systematic tracking of shifts in funders' priorities and setting specific numerical goals concerning city coalitions. The elephant in the room discussion was also not forgotten. We were defining food insecurity and food justice interchangeably. We needed to know how they were being defined in the field and in practice. We pursued this path in Planning for the Future.

In essence, the dialogue was engaging. It highlighted key activities that needed to be tracked and addressed throughout the empowerment evaluation. The evidence and series of suggestions for improvement were used in the Planning for the Future step of the engagement.

Planning for the Future (Abbreviated)

Equitable Food Access members of the empowerment evaluation teams built on the Taking Stock step of the process by generating a Plan for the Future. It was based on their ratings and dialogue, and consisted of

The Plan for the Future consisted of specified goals (drawn from the list of activities rated and discussed), strategies (drawn from the evidence provided for the ratings in the Taking Stock step), and evidence (to verify that the strategies were being implemented and were effective).

specified goals (drawn from the list of activities that were rated and discussed), strategies (drawn from the evidence provided for the ratings in the Taking Stock step), and evidence (to verify that the strategies were being implemented and were effective). An example is provided in Figure 3.5.

A few draft Plans for the Future were discussed in detail during the empowerment evaluation exercise, specifically "Identify partners who can amplify and broaden your engagement" and "Seek and gather feedback from communities we serve to identify inclusive best practices."

A subgroup was also assembled to explore how food insecurity, food justice, and food sovereignty were defined. Food insecurity and security are typically defined by government agencies like the USDA and are focused on charitable giving and on the amounts of food that are distributed. Food justice and sovereignty were generally defined by equity movements and/or organizations, focusing on justice, entitlement, and

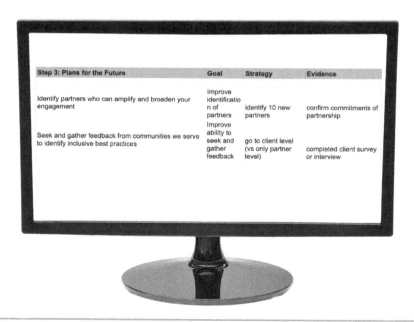

Step 3: Plans for the Future	Goal	Strategy	Evidence
Identify partners who can amplify and broaden your engagement	Improve identification of partners	identify 10 new partners	confirm commitments of partnership
Seek and gather feedback from communities we serve to identify inclusive best practices	Improve ability to seek and gather feedback	go to client level (vs only partner level)	completed client survey or interview

FIGURE 3.5. Plans for the Future. Example of a Plan for the Future with the goals, strategies, and evidence listed.

human rights. Temporary working definitions were prepared and are presented in the following list:

- *Food insecurity*—Lack of consistent access to enough food for every person in a household to live an active and healthy life.
- *Food security*—Both physical and economic access to sufficient food to meet dietary needs for a productive and healthy life.
- *Food justice*—Healthy food is viewed as a human right. The movement was founded to combat structural racism and access to resources, focusing on the distribution of food within low-income communities. The larger politics of food production are not always challenged.
- *Food sovereignty*—Healthy and culturally appropriate food is also viewed as a human right. In addition, people have the right to determine their own food and agricultural production systems. The movement was founded by peasant farmers and calls for equal and democratized food production systems. In addition, food should be produced using ecologically sound and sustainable methods.

These definitions helped grantees evaluate their performance by explicitly stating their overarching goals.

Alignment and Integration with the Preexisting Evaluation Questions

Grantees' Taking Stock and Planning for the Future activities opened up the floodgates. One of their activities was "seeking and gathering feedback from communities they served." Their preexisting survey questions were now viewed with an eye toward how they might respond to their empowerment evaluation questions. They linked their Plans for the Future with many of the preexisting survey questions, contextualizing and repurposing the same questions. A few of the examples are provided in Table 3.1.

The role of Starbucks was arguably one of the most important questions in the evaluation. It was also one of the most ambiguous. It could take any shape from using neighborhood Starbucks stores for meetings or distributions centers to educating Starbucks employees about food-security-related issues.

TABLE 3.1. Aligning Empowerment Evaluation Plans with Preexisting Survey Questions

Empowerment Evaluation Plans for the Future	Preexisting Survey Questions
Increasing the Number of Partners	How many partners do you have now?
	How many more partners do you plan to have by the end of the year?
Building More Coalitions	How many coalitions do you plan to establish this year?
Building Starbucks Relationships	Provide examples of food bank relationships and activities with Starbucks stores in your neighborhood.
Improving Organizational Policies to Be More Equitable	How do your organizational policies impact communities of color?
Spending More Time with "Boots on the Ground"	What kinds of food would you like to have available?
	When (what time of the year) would you like to have these foods available?
	What foods would you not like to see in the food banks?
	How challenging is finding a site for free meals and/or groceries that is open during the times or days of the week when you need it?
	How often have you had trouble accessing free meals and/or groceries because: • You did not have easy access to a car or public transit • You couldn't afford gas or transit fare • You had trouble carrying your food home • The location was unsafe
Assessing Needs	What is the size of your BIPOC community in need of assistance?
	Are you reaching the BIPOC community? If so, how do you know?
	How many people are served in the BIPOC community?
Improving Representativeness	How many BIPOC members of the community work at your food bank?
	How many BIPOC members of the community are on your food bank board?
	What percent of the growers are members of the BIPOC community?
	How many more BIPOC growers are you planning to help contribute to food security in the community?

The empowerment evaluation provided grantees with an opportunity to clarify their Plans for the Future, operationalize them, and link them to preexisting survey questions. One of Food Bank for New York City's Plans for the Future is provided in the following list and includes the Food Bank's goal, strategies, and evidence.

Goal

Increase SNAP outreach in high-needs, food-insecure BIPOC communities in NYC.

Strategies

1. Identify key member and partner locations of high need within a reasonable radius of Starbucks Community Store locations.
2. Enlist and train Starbucks Community Store employees to support SNAP outreach.
3. Host Starbucks employees at community outreach events at FB member sites.
4. Survey clients to understand the barriers to SNAP participation for likely eligible Black participants.

Evidence

1. the number of Black- and Latino-led member agencies in a walkable radius from Starbucks Community Stores
2. the number of Starbucks staff trainings held
3. the number of Starbucks employees trained
4. the number of outreach events conducted
5. the number of Starbucks employees participating
6. the number of clients engaged in SNAP outreach
7. the number of client surveys administered
8. a qualitative analysis of survey results

These very specific lists of strategies and evidence were further linked with preexisting (and often very general and open-ended) survey questions, such as provide examples of food bank relationships and activities with Starbucks stores in your neighborhood. Instead of providing equally vague responses to this general question, grantees were able to provide strategic, and almost surgically precise, responses that were relevant and meaningful to them.

Linking Survey Responses to Plans for the Future

The link between their empowerment evaluation Plans for the Future exercise and Feeding America's preexisting survey is powerfully illustrated by the grantees' use of the survey responses. For example, one of their empowerment evaluation Plans for the Future goals was "Spending More Time with Boots on the Ground." This goal was linked with the following preexisting survey question, "How challenging is finding a site for free meals/groceries that is open during the times or days of the week when you need it?"

The survey results documented that 59% of the Food Bank survey respondents were challenged finding a site for free meals/groceries open during the times or days of the week when they needed them (see Figure 3.6). It was clear that too many people found it challenging and improvements were needed. This was important to know before launching a campaign to fix things.

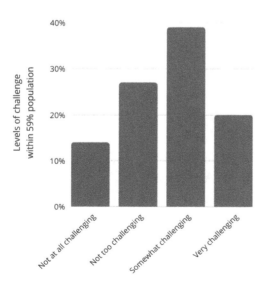

FIGURE 3.6. Fifty-nine percent of Food Bank survey respondents were challenged to find a site for free meals or groceries.

This survey finding raised the question "Who found it challenging?" It was time to apply a racial equity lens to this question (see Feeding America, 2022). A simple sort of Food Bank survey respondents by race/ethnicity answered that fundamental and important question: 31% Black, 29% White, 12% Asian, 1% American Indian, 0.5% Native Hawaiian, and 0.5% Middle Eastern (see Figure 3.7).

The answer to that question led to another question, so they had to dig deeper. They knew who they were serving based on racial/ethnic identity. Now they needed to know how difficult each ethnic group experienced finding a site that was open during a time that worked for them. They returned to the survey data and sorted for "race/ethnicity" and "who found it somewhat or very challenging." A comparison between ethnic groups was illuminating. The percent finding it "somewhat" or "very challenging" was: Asian 80%, American Indian 69%, Black 48%, and White 59% (see Figure 3.8).

The survey responses created a standard, or yardstick, across food banks. Individual food banks could compare their survey respondents with this racial equity standard to determine where they stood in terms of service to their communities. The survey data became meaningful, if not invaluable. Instead of being viewed as a preexisting, academic, and irrelevant requirement of the grant, the survey responses were reframed. The survey responses answered relevant questions that food bank members were asking with a racial/ethnic equity lens.

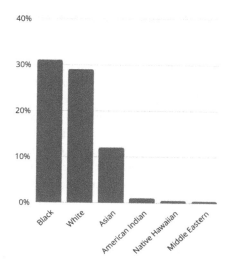

FIGURE 3.7. Racial/ethnic distribution across food banks.

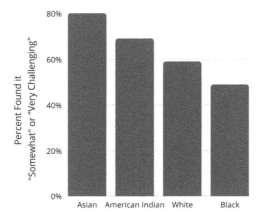

FIGURE 3.8. Degree of challenge by racial/ethnic group.

Evaluation Dashboards

The next step after completing the three-step empowerment evaluation exercise and linking it to preexisting (but now relevant and contextualized) survey questions was to create evaluation dashboards. They were used to monitor progress toward new goals or proposed Planning for the Future interventions. The dashboards included baselines, goals, milestones, and actual performance. The actual performance was compared with the milestones to monitor and document progress toward annual and longer-term goals.

> The evaluation dashboards included baselines, goals, milestones, and actual performance.

Evaluation dashboards were designed to monitor both numerical and descriptive data. For example, one evaluation dashboard was used to monitor and record the number of trainings provided. Another dashboard described specific activities required in a logical sequence to accomplish the group's goals, for example, quarter one—identify the range of clients to interview and survey; quarter two—pilot interview protocols and specify communities; quarter three—conduct surveys and interviews with clients (as compared with partners); quarter four—identify patterns, summarize findings, and report on findings and recommendations.

An evaluation dashboard is presented in Figure 3.9. It is based on the group's Plan for the Future goal: "Increase the number of partnerships." This evaluation dashboard provides the following information:

Actual performance: TBD each quarter

Milestones: 1 new partnership in quarter 1, 5 in quarter 2, 7 in quarter 3, and 10 at year end

Goal: Establish 10 new partnerships this year

These evaluation dashboards provided Equitable Food Access grantees with a tool to monitor their performance toward quarterly and annual goals. These dashboard tables and bar charts (see Figure 3.10) also helped grantees make midcourse corrections when strategies were not helping the group accomplish its goals.

Viewing Donors as Change Agents

The authenticity, pace, and meaning of this entire endeavor is in the hands of the community. However, it is shaped and influenced administratively and financially from the top. Funding agencies that are philosophically aligned with an empowerment evaluation approach help

	Q1	Q2	Q3	Q4
Actual Performance	1			
Milestones	1	5	7	10
Goal	10	10	10	10

FIGURE 3.9. Evaluation dashboard table.

FIGURE 3.10. Evaluation dashboard bar chart.

ensure its integrity, support capacity building, leverage existing resources, and encourage innovation.

Advocate

Funding agencies that are philosophically aligned with an empowerment evaluation approach help ensure its integrity, support capacity building, leverage existing resources, and encourage innovation.

Dr. Tom Summerfelt, Vice President and Chief Research Officer at Feeding America (see Figure 3.11), was an advocate for the food banks. He identified the need for an evaluation approach that was responsive to their concerns. He took the initiative to identify an evaluator and a stakeholder involvement approach that was in alignment with Feeding America and Starbuck's philosophical orientation toward programs and evaluations.

Dr. Summerfelt orchestrated introductions, legitimized stakeholder involvement, and facilitated capacity building. He also ensured that funding was allocated for the empowerment evaluation.

FIGURE 3.11. Drs. David Fetterman and Tom Summerfelt exploring conceptual crossroads, focusing on the integration of the empowerment evaluation and the preexisting evaluation plans.

Racial Equity Lens

Dr. Summerfelt also recognized the need for technical assistance, specifically helping the food banks apply a racial equity lens to their work. He recruited Dr. Angela Odoms-Young, a food and nutrition equity evaluation specialist from Cornell and Visiting Equity Scholar at Feeding America. She helped the evaluation team and food bank grantees adopt and apply a racial equity lens.

Politically Adept

Dr. Summerfelt was also politically adept. He was sensitive to the food bank's concerns and at the same time understood both what was needed and what was possible at Feeding America. He successfully navigated the organizational currents in order to manage the project. He was responsible for securing "approval" from Feeding America to shift gears. In addition, he managed the introductions concerning the approach to his evaluation team, Starbucks' grantees, and Starbucks' management.

Interpersonal Skills

Dr. Summerfelt is a collaborative, self-reflective, and forward-thinking leader. His interpersonal skills are finely honed. He is genuine in his praise for team member contributions. He also has the ability to speak frankly, but in a friendly and inviting manner, communicating clearly about his needs as a leader. Moreover, he demonstrated a respect for grantees' knowledge, experience, and self-determination.

During one of the transitions in the empowerment evaluation in which evaluation dashboards and survey data were being aligned, he met with each of the grantees individually. He took the time to reassure them that this was their evaluation. He repeatedly asked them what they wanted to know, instead of telling them what would meet funding requirements.

Reflective Instead of Deflected

Dr. Summerfelt also was capable of regrouping and reassessing their initial efforts. Feeding America experienced significant push back from grantees when they first introduced the standardized module of survey questions required for funding that we discussed earlier. The aim in general was to come up with a single set of questions that applied to all food bank evaluations. In response to their resistance, he reflected, instead of deflected. He openly acknowledged the need to reassess the evaluation process.

> "We need to make sure this (survey) works for you. That's why we have invited David to help us connect the dots and make this evaluation as useful to you as possible, while acknowledging we have made promises to Starbucks."

One of the Feeding America's administrators made the organization's position even more explicit: "We made a mistake. We have failed to answer your questions about (the survey), but we will fix that. Now we need to pivot."

Organizational and Infrastructural Support

David Duguid, former Director of Evaluation, Adriana Riaño, Program Manager, Hollie Baker-Lutz, former Director of Equitable Access, and Bria Berger, Research Manager, all at Feeding America, organized and orchestrated internal weekly meetings and quarterly conferences with grantees. This organizational and infrastructural support provided both consistency and continuity to the evaluation. It also provided the conceptual guidance and brainstorming required to maximize the time needed to work productively with food bank grantees.

Moreover, although the entire evaluation team enthusiastically embraced the stakeholder involvement approach, the team grounded us in the preexisting contractual agreements for conducting the surveys. Once they learned about the grantee resistance to the surveys, they were willing to stop what they were doing and use the empowerment evaluation approach to help make the surveys more meaningful and relevant. Basically, they saw the logic of restarting the evaluation from the grantees' perspective and needs. This allowed the grantees to reframe the usefulness and value of the preexisting surveys by making them more relevant and responsive to grantee questions about their effectiveness.

The donor change agents literally set the tone for an empowerment evaluation from the top down by valuing views from the bottom up. They offered the empowerment evaluation as a tool to help the food banks take charge of their own evaluation, recognizing the need to have a greater stakeholder involvement approach. This enabled them to make the questions meaningful and useful, linking their Plan for the Future with many of the preexisting questions.

> The donor change agents literally set the tone for an empowerment evaluation from the top down by valuing views from the bottom up.

CONCLUSION

This chapter provides a real-world application of a large-scale empowerment evaluation. It highlights how empowerment evaluation places much of the evaluation in the hands of the community or, in this case, grantees. The grantees monitored their own progress and conducted their own assessments of their efforts, rather than having the evaluation done for them. This created more buy-in or ownership, contributing to its usefulness.

This discussion also demonstrates how a racial equity or racial justice lens can be used to shape organizational (and, in this case, food bank) practices. This ranged from ensuring that communities of color were served to ensuring that minority members worked at the food banks with the hope of serving on food bank boards.

> This brief case example demonstrates how an empowerment evaluation was conducted within the context of a preexisting contractually agreed-upon evaluation plan. The Equitable Food Access team, change agents in their own right, contributed to the creation of powerful change agents in the community. They helped establish community-owned mechanisms to monitor and eliminate food insecurity.

Fundamentally, however, this brief case example demonstrates how an empowerment evaluation was conducted within the context of a preexisting contractually agreed-upon evaluation plan. In this case the metrics preceded the purpose. The survey questions were well designed and had the appropriate intent. However, members of the food banks did not own those questions. The empowerment evaluation approach helped everyone take two steps back before helping to make the preexisting metrics relevant and meaningful to the community of grantees (and minimize pushing back against external data collection efforts).

Integrating Empowerment Evaluation within a Preexisting Workplan and Celebrating Donors as Change Agents

USAID/REACH's Initiative
to Eliminate Tuberculosis in India

> *Life is a process of reduction, starting with the largest dream and ending with the smallest steps to get you there.*

C hapter 3, on Feeding America's fight for food justice in the United States, responded to the question of whether an empowerment evaluation can be conducted when there is a preexisting evaluation framework and specific requirements. This chapter responds to a similar question: Can an empowerment evaluation be conducted when there is a preexisting workplan in place?

The response, paralleling that in the previous chapter, is yes. An empowerment evaluation can ground the existing workplan in community concerns, priorities, and issues, making programmatic implementation more credible and ultimately more sustainable. It is designed to reinforce and guide program implementation efforts. An empowerment evaluation often enhances the existing workplan and expands the scope, depth, or breadth of the program services.

Similar to an empowerment evaluation within a preexisting framework, discussed in the previous chapter, an empowerment evaluation in the context of a preexisting workplan can make the routine and somewhat

> An empowerment evaluation can ground the existing workplan in community concerns, priorities, and issues, making programmatic implementation more credible and ultimately more sustainable.

burdensome program implementation tasks more meaningful, relevant, and necessary. An empowerment evaluation can be used to reframe existing program implementation tasks, transforming them from the trivial and mundane to the essential and exciting.

STEPPING IN TO REFRAME, REFINE, AND RESTORE PREEXISTING WORKPLANS

An empowerment evaluation is similar to looking at the same problem with a fresh set of eyes, specifically the community's or stakeholders' eyes, instead of from the evaluator's, administrator's, or sponsor's perspectives. Revisiting the Mission helps a community group recalibrate and reassert what the group's priorities are and its purpose and reason for being. It can restore a group or a workplan back to its original intent. Taking Stock provides people with the opportunity to reflect on their work (or workplan) and refine it—making the workplan more precise, strategic, and surgical in terms of its ability to precisely identify and address needs and remove obstacles. Planning for the Future provides the context in which to reframe the workplan activities and make them more meaningful, functional, and valued. This United States Agency for International Development (USAID)-funded empowerment evaluation to eliminate tuberculosis in India provides insight into the dynamics of integrating empowerment evaluation into a preexisting workplan.

> An empowerment evaluation is similar to looking at the same problem with a fresh set of eyes, specifically the community's or stakeholders' eyes, instead of from the evaluator's, administrator's, or sponsor's perspectives.

PROGRAM AND INITIATIVE DESCRIPTION

Tuberculosis (TB) is both preventable and curable, yet remains among the top 10 causes of death globally. India has 27% of the total TB burden. It has the most deaths due to TB and the greatest number of people with drug-resistant TB. The government of India has committed to eliminating TB by 2025, prior to the UN global target. The USAID has pioneered engaging communities to help eliminate TB in India.

> Tuberculosis (TB) is both preventable and curable, yet remains among the top 10 causes of death globally.

The Resource Group for Education and Advocacy for Community Health (REACH) is using a USAID-funded empowerment evaluation approach to accomplish its objectives, focusing on the Accountability Leadership by Local Communities for Inclusive, Enabling Services (ALLIES) project. The ALLIES project aims to enable environments for TB elimination through community empowerment by

- establishing community-owned mechanisms to monitor the quality of TB care and services and give feedback to the program for timely responses,
- ensuring sustainability by generating local solutions through patient literacy on rights, behavioral change counseling, and referrals to services,
- creating powerful advocates at multiple levels to shape rights-respectful and accountable TB services, and
- promoting policy, regulatory, and financial environments that support TB elimination at the state and national levels among parliamentarians and decision makers.

Empowerment evaluation was designed to help determine if the ALLIES project was on course, diverging, and/or changing life for the better. Empowerment evaluation created an honest and open space for dialogue, self-critique, and learning for the ALLIES project. REACH's empowerment evaluation dashboard of TB Rights-Based Training highlights how empowerment evaluation tools have been used in the field.

This case example matches a community-based initiative to eliminate TB with a community-based evaluation approach. It also demonstrates how empowerment evaluation can be used to help people monitor and assess their own performance.

STEPS TO INTEGRATE EMPOWERMENT EVALUATION INTO PREEXISTING WORKPLANS

The three-step empowerment evaluation approach was selected because it was in alignment with REACH's philosophical orientation and in part because of its simplicity, effectiveness, transparency, and sustainability. REACH conducted a series of empowerment evaluation exercises in order to reestablish goals, monitor progress, make midcourse corrections, and accomplish its objectives over time.

COVID complicated the logistics and created delays. Natural hesitancies and insecurities were apparent, creating additional delays. There were tensions between the policy-driven aspirations to move forward more rapidly and the practice groups operating "on the ground." The practice groups were aware of practical logistics and were hesitant to "disrupt existing relationships between health care providers and TB Champions or advocates." However, the core team remained focused, persistent, and on target. National and state groups conducted empowerment evaluations within the context of existing workplan requirements. Team members reflected on their practice and progress. "Game-changer" ideas and activities emerged, reshaping both program implementation and the corresponding empowerment evaluation.

> "Game changer" ideas and activities emerged as we engaged in dialogue, reshaping both program implementation and the corresponding empowerment evaluation.

CONDUCTING THE THREE STEPS

We launched the three steps on a national and then on a state level. The same three-step approach was later practiced on a local level. The approach was conducted with each group and involved (1) facilitating a discussion about the group's Mission; (2) prioritizing the list of activities that made the Mission possible and then rating each activity and dialoguing about each one; and (3) Planning for the Future, with specific goals (drawn from the Taking Stock list of activities), strategies (drawn from the specific evidence shared during the Taking Stock rating dialogue), and evidence.

The exercises solidified and strengthened the initiative by reducing and narrowing the scope of the intervention. The mantra became *do more by doing less.* The Mission represented the most expansive level of the initiative. The prioritization step of Taking Stock rapidly reduced the scope of the effort. The Planning for the Future step was like a mining expedition, digging deep to unearth gems. The step represented a quantum leap in terms of reducing or narrowing the scope to a few critical activities. It allowed the group to maximize the "dose effect" by concentrating its efforts on a few absolutely critical activities.

> The mantra became *do more by doing less.*

The evaluation dashboards were used to help the group monitor its own performance, make midcourse corrections, and ultimately reach its goals. This case example in India illustrates how empowerment evaluation can function within an existing workplan and enhance its quality and impact.

> Empowerment evaluation allowed the group to maximize the "dose effect" by concentrating its efforts on a few absolutely critical activities.

USAID/REACH AND TB ELIMINATION: A CASE EXAMPLE

REACH colleagues posted key phrases reflecting their Mission on Google Sheets. This exercise helped them come to a consensus concerning their Mission or values. It also crystalized a shared vision of what was important to them and where they wanted to go. A few selected phrases include:

Mission Statements

- Building the capacity of health care providers to view and work with communities as ALLIES for TB elimination
- Advocating for better policies within the health care system
- Supporting and capacity building of affected communities and/or TB survivors for community-engagement activities
- Training of frontline health care providers on soft skills
- Helping TB survivors become movers and shakers in the TB program
- Training TB survivors and Champions in rights-based approaches
- Promoting human-centered care by consciously putting people at the center of all that we do
- Generating local solutions to address the issues of people with TB

These phrases were later used to develop a Mission statement:

The End TB mission is a priority of the government of India and REACH jointly with NTEP [National Tuberculosis Elimination Programme] in this endeavor. REACH envisages its role in eliminating TB in India through engaging the people with TB and the health providers, including private practitioners. As highlighted in the National Strategic Plan 2017–2025, engaging TB survivors and building their capacity to stand for their rights, represent their community, and demand respectful and rights-based TB care and treatment will enable a better environment for communities with TB. On the other hand, REACH also supports the TB-elimination program by engaging the health care providers through capacity building and sensitization so that they provide improved care and support services and see communities as an active participants in the government health system. REACH also aims at creating an enabling environment through policy advocacy for a multisectoral partnership approach where providers and communities work hand in hand for TB elimination.

Taking Stock I (Brainstorming and Prioritization)

After reaching a consensus about the Mission, group members evaluated their efforts (within the context of a set of shared values). First they brainstormed and generated a list of some of the most important activities required to accomplish organizational, programmatic, and educational goals (contributing to their Mission). Then, using the five-vote approach, they prioritized the list of activities in terms of what group members thought were the most important to evaluate as a group from that point on in the evaluation (see Figures 4.1 and 4.2). The activities included:

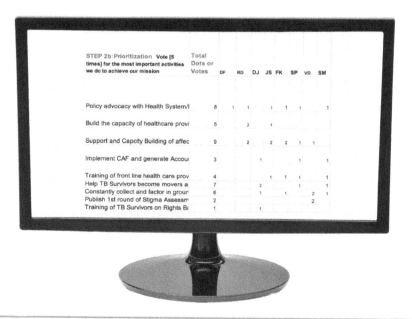

FIGURE 4.1. Prioritization. "Voting" for the most important activities to rate, discuss, and evaluate. Total votes in are in the left middle column, and individual votes are in the right columns.

- Policy advocacy with health care system
- Building the capacity of health care providers to view and work with communities as allies for TB elimination
- Implementing the Community Accountability Framework (CAF) and generating accountability reports
- Supporting and capacity building of affected communities and/ or TB survivors for community-engagement activities; capacity building of TB Champions
- Training of frontline health care providers on soft skills
- Constantly collecting and factoring in ground-level feedback from the state program managers and district TB strategists to shape the way to do things
- Helping TB survivors become movers and shakers in the TB program

FIGURE 4.2. Prioritization graph. Graphically highlighting the results of the prioritization exercise.

- Publishing the first round of stigma-assessment findings
- Training TB survivors on rights-based approaches

Taking Stock II (Rating and Dialogue)

REACH colleagues selected nine activities to rate, discuss, and evaluate during the first empowerment evaluation exercise. They rated how well they were performing each of the activities selected, using a scale of 1 (low) to 10 (high). The columns were averaged horizontally and vertically. In the vertical column, the group could see who was typically optimistic and/or pessimistic. This helped the group calibrate or evaluate the ratings and opinions of each individual member. It also helped the group establish norms. In the horizontal column, the averages provided the group with a consolidated view of how well (or poorly) each activity was being performed. A selection of the group's ratings using Google Sheets is presented in Figures 4.3 and 4.4.

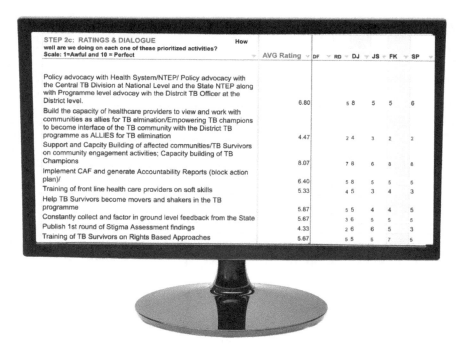

FIGURE 4.3. Ratings. Average ratings are in the center column. Individual ratings using a scale of 1 (low) to 10 (high) are in the right-hand columns.

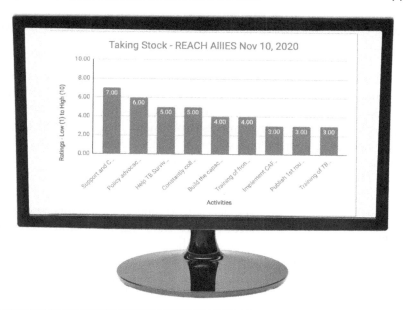

FIGURE 4.4. Ratings graph. Graphically highlighting the results of the rating exercise.

The activities receiving the highest ratings during the second exercise included:

- Supporting and capacity building of affected communities and/or TB survivors for community engagement activities
- Policy advocacy with health care system
- Implementing CAF and generating accountability reports (block action plan)

The activities receiving the lowest ratings included:

- Publishing the first round of stigma-assessment findings
- Enlisting communities as allies of TB elimination and training and empowering TB Champions

The empowerment evaluation Taking Stock May ratings were compared with the November ratings. Significant gains were made in each area. The most significant increases concerned *implementing CAF and generating accountability reports (block action plan)* and *training TB survivors on rights-based approaches.*

Their dialogue highlighted some of the key activities that needed to be tracked through the empowerment evaluation. The empowerment evaluators inquired about the rationale for the ratings and asked what it would take for REACH to assign higher ratings for each activity. This question prompted group members to outline the steps that they believed were needed to improve the program's impact. These steps were included in the Planning for the Future step of the engagement.

The dialogue about the ratings was one of the most important parts of the process. In addition to clarifying issues, evidence was used during the dialogue to support viewpoints, and "sensitive topics" were surfaced and examined. Moreover, the process of specifying the reason or evidence for a rating provided the group with a more efficient and focused manner of identifying what needed to be done next during the Planning for the Future step of the process. Instead of generating an unwieldy list of strategies and solutions that may or may not have been relevant to the issues at hand, the group was able to focus its energies on the specific concerns and reasons for a low rating that were raised in the dialogue or exchange. The bar graphs in Figure 4.5 compare ratings across two formal Taking Stock exercises over a 7-month period.

> The process of specifying the reason or evidence for a rating provided the group with a more efficient and focused manner of identifying what needed to be done next during the Planning for the Future step of the process.

Planning for the Future

The first Taking Stock step represented baseline ratings that were compared with the ratings in the second Taking Stock exercise. A comparison of the group ratings over time helped REACH members measure their progress toward specified goals. After rating and discussing programmatic activities, the members specified Plans for the Future in both exercises (see Figure 4.6). This step involved generating goals, strategies, and credible evidence to determine if the strategies were being implemented and if they were effective.

> A comparison of the group ratings over time helped REACH members measure their progress toward specified goals.

The goals were directly related to the activities selected in the Taking Stock step. For example, since the activity "Build the capacity of

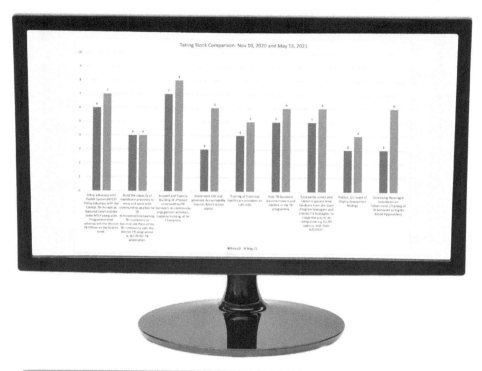

FIGURE 4.5. Graph comparing Taking Stock ratings (7-month period).

health care providers to view and work with communities as allies for TB elimination" was prioritized, rated, and discussed, then improving it became one of the goals. The strategies emerged from the Taking Stock discussion as well.

For example, one of the reasons given for the low ratings involved cultural barriers to the need for enhancing capacity. Recommended strategies for addressing this concern included breaking down cultural barriers by asking health care providers and TB Champions to attend the same empowerment evaluation–capacity building meetings.

The goal of mentoring TB Champions was addressed by pursuing specific strategies, such as using the Grow, Reality, Options, and Will (GROW) coaching model. Specific evidence was also listed to determine if the strategies were being implemented and in fact were making a difference, for example, in whether TB survivors were receiving appropriate treatment.

STEP 3: PLAN FOR THE FUTURE ("Activities" in "Taking Stock" inform "Goals"; "Evidence" in "Taking Stock" (during dialogue about ratings) inform "Strategies"	Goals	Strategies	Evidence
			TB Champions demonstrating assertiveness with health care providers; TB Champions and health care providers reporting
Mentor TB Champions to interact with health system to resolve gaps in a healthy and non confrontational manner	Create and improve mentorship of TB Champions to interact with health syastem to resolve gaps in a health and non confronrational manner	Use the GROW model to coach TB Champions	constructive interactions; TB patients and survivors feeling heard and receiving appropriate treatment

FIGURE 4.6. Example of a Plan for the Future with a goal, strategy, and evidence.

Alignment with the Workplan

Once the three-step process was complete, each Plan for the Future and evaluation dashboard were aligned with REACH's existing workplan. This is precisely where empowerment evaluation was integrated into the group's existing set of commitments and planned activities. The workplan became more meaningful because it was now embedded within REACH's staff members' goals and strategies (which were derived from their empowerment evaluation exercises).

> The workplan became more meaningful because it was now embedded within REACH's staff members' goals and strategies (which were derived from their empowerment evaluation exercises).

For example, the workplan called for training 250 health care staff in "soft skills" by the end of the year. It involved training "TB survivors in target project districts on a rights-based curriculum that equips them with the awareness and know-how about the rights and entitlements of a person who is living with or has had TB. The curriculum covers sensitive areas like notification, confidentiality, quarantining, and interface with health system."

This workplan matched the empowerment evaluation goal of conducting rights-based training among TB survivors and TB-affected community members to create a cadre of rights-aware community volunteers. Strategies to achieve this goal included:

- Advocating to get the rights-based curriculum approved
- Designing an operational plan to roll out the training, including identifying community members and TB survivors who will play a crucial role in implementing the training
- Conducting trainings at regular intervals
- Planning for a follow-up action module for people trained in the rights-based curriculum
- Conducting mock dialogues with health care providers about a series of "difficult" problems that needed to be addressed (with the expectation that the TB Champions use some of the tools or resources learned from the training)
- Documenting or recording how well staff members interacted with the health care providers they worked with

REACH staff members also agreed on the need for credible evidence to document that they were conducting these strategies and that they were in fact effective. The evidence they considered included:

- Producing a finalized rights-based curriculum
- Creating an operational planning document with state teams
- Conducting pre- and posttraining assessments for each group trained
- Producing the results of mock dialogue sessions (with high, medium, and low self-evaluation ratings and ratings from one of our team members)

Evaluation Dashboards

Evaluation dashboards were developed to help REACH team members monitor their progress on a quarterly basis. This monitoring enabled them to make midcourse corrections as needed, revise their strategies, and more closely approximate their milestones and goals.

> Evaluation dashboards were developed to help REACH team members monitor their progress on a quarterly basis.

The evaluation dashboards also helped staff members monitor their progress on activities that they thought were critical to accomplish their Mission. Those same activities were now in alignment with their contractually agreed upon workplan. An example is presented in Figures 4.7 and 4.8.

Actual performance: the actual number of community members trained on rights-based curriculum in each quarter.

Milestones: milestones planned were 0 or NA in Q1, 100 in Q2, 200 in Q3, and 250 in Q4.

Goals: 250 community members across four project states by the end of Y2.

Baseline: the number of community members trained prior to establishing this plan.

The REACH's ALLIES Initiative made significant strides concerning each Taking Stock activity selected by the group. In addition, Dr. Jayalakshmi Shreedhar, health journalist and medical doctor, and REACH recommended the application of the empowerment evaluation approach "all the way down the line to the implementation teams and TB Champions."

Subrat Mohanty, a senior advisor at REACH and project leader at ALLIES, and I agreed with this recommendation. TB Champions and others at the local level could use the same approach to assess their own performance. Mohanty also recommended that the team use the approach with all levels of REACH to help develop the year three plan. REACH is incorporating empowerment evaluation reports into its monthly meetings. A ripple effect has already occurred whereby other groups, such as Touched by TB, have expressed an interest in applying the approach to improve their performance in similar initiatives designed to eliminate TB in India.

The selection of the empowerment evaluation approach is in alignment with the initiative, both philosophically and in practice. The convergence of values and principles made this an excellent match with far-ranging implications for additional multistate implementation. In addition, the use of this tool is serving to accelerate REACH's progress toward its desired and stated goals.

> The evaluation dashboard is serving to accelerate REACH's progress toward its desired and stated goals.

	1st Quarter	2nd Quarter	3rd Quarter	4th Quarter
Actual Performance	NA			
Milestone	NA	100	200	250
Goals	NA	250	250	250
Baseline	NA	0	0	0

FIGURE 4.7. Evaluation dashboard table.

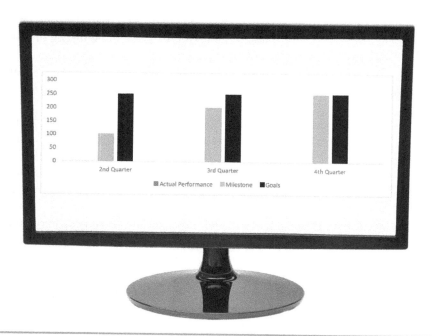

FIGURE 4.8. Evaluation dashboard bar chart.

REACH is contributing to the creation of powerful change agents, establishing community-owned mechanisms to monitor TB care and service, to generate local solutions, to promote discourse, and to establish accountability. The REACH's ALLIES project is on a promising path to help to eliminate TB and reduce TB-related stigmatization and discrimination, creating healthier communities throughout India.

The Role of Donors as Change Agents

One of the least common but most important questions in empowerment evaluation is: What's the role of the donor? All too often, the donor's role is too narrowly defined. One classic characterization of donors is that they leave the money by the door and disappear until the end of the project. They return only to ask the same questions posed at the beginning of the project. However, life changes and projects evolve over time. Ideally learning occurs, programs adapt and pivot to remain responsive to community changes and needs, and outcomes need to be renegotiated to make sense and remain relevant.

Donors need to stay in touch with the program or initiative from beginning to end. They need to participate in (not control) the decision-making process at every stage of the journey. This participation minimizes the classic problem of being out of touch with the adaptations required, holding grantees to outdated or irrelevant outcomes, and "pulling the rug out from under" the grantee by adhering to antiquated expectations.

> Donors need to stay in touch with the program or initiative from beginning to end.

Program staff and community members also need to rethink the role of donors. Instead of viewing donors as benevolent investors, program and community members (and evaluators) could benefit from viewing them in terms of their knowledge about their vast array of community investments. Donors can make an important contribution to learning, as well as to accountability.

Many donors value learning, self-determination, and capacity building. They are philosophically aligned with empowerment evaluation principles. The funding officer plays a pivotal role in lobbying for an empowerment evaluation. She or he typically recruits the empowerment evaluation team and also introduces the empowerment evaluation team to the project team or community members, so they can determine if there is a good fit.

> The funding officer plays a pivotal role in lobbying for an empowerment evaluation.

This brief summary of a USAID-sponsored REACH initiative to eliminate TB in India provides insight into the complex and substantive role a good steward can play in the development and success of a program, initiative, or community effort.

Advocates

Amrita Goswami and Kachina Chawla were USAID empowerment evaluation advocates and change agents (see Figure 4.9). They recognized the alignment between empowerment evaluation principles and practices and REACH's grass roots approach to change. They made the introductions between the empowerment evaluators and the REACH implementation and evaluation team members. They also secured the

FIGURE 4.9. Amrita Goswami and Kachina Chawla serving as critical donor friends.

funding for the empowerment evaluation to supplement and complement the existing evaluation framework and program implementation efforts.

Attuned to National Policy

Amrita and Kachina were also attuned to significant shifts in national policy, which were aligned with empowerment evaluation's principles. At the End TB Summit in Delhi, India's Prime Minister Narendra Modi (2018) acknowledged, "We have not been successful in curbing tuberculosis yet. I believe that if something doesn't yield results even after 10–15 years then we need to change our approach." He announced the launch of the TB-Free India Campaign at the summit. The change he was referring to was the "dawn of the community-led response for TB in India" (Sachdeva, 2020, p. 266). According to Kuldeep Singh Sachdeva (2020), "Empowering people with TB and their communities through effective social mobilization, is now being implemented systematically in the TB programme. The contribution of community has been recognized as a cost-effective intervention to improve coverage of health services and deliver people-centric integrated care" (p. 266). J. P. Nadda, Union health minister, also confirmed that "community engagement is the hallmark and it is becoming a social movement to end TB in India" (Sharma, 2018). Amrita and Kachina, guided by this shift in national policy, were instrumental in directing resources to the local level in India, pertaining to both programmatic and evaluative tasks. They valued placing evaluation in the hands of community and program staff members.

> "Empowering people with TB and their communities through effective social mobilization is now being implemented systematically in the TB programme. The contribution of community has been recognized as a cost-effective intervention to improve coverage of health services and deliver people-centric integrated care" (Sachdeva, p. 266).

Recognized Opportunity

They also saw a window of opportunity to help transform USAID in the process. Senior USAID leadership, much like the Indian prime minister, was tired of experiencing the limitations of the existing methods and recognized the need to try something new. This evaluation served in part as a test case. The success of the program and evaluation helped to inform and transform USAID evaluation practice, which had not substantially changed in decades.

These change agents were articulate, thoughtful, and experienced leaders. They had a vision of the potential they were helping to unleash and actualize. They were risk takers, in that they were willing to place their careers and reputation on the line for what they believed to be the "right path" for India.

Critical Friend

Kachina in particular played the role of the supportive critical friend on many occasions. She served as a "cheerleader" complimenting and reinforcing each of us along the way. For example, after a brief webinar that was part of the dissemination plan, she complimented and encouraged each member of the team:

> Hi All,
>
> I just wanted to say that in preparing for this webinar what I realized is the brilliance of each and every one of you on this team. You are all trailblazers in your own way. Rahul and Catherine—thanks for leading us on this journey and David, thanks for being the guiding star. Sandip, thanks for pushing us to always think broader on where else and how this can work. Subrat, thank you for creating the enabling environment at REACH where such an idea can flourish. Amrita, thanks for believing in the process and being willing to challenge the status quo at USAID/India.
>
> This has been a delightful learning journey for me but also for the agency. On the webinar yesterday we had at least six USAID MEL people [responsible for monitoring, evaluation, and learning] from across the globe and other offices. Collectively, I do believe you have initiated a long-needed cycle of change—well done!!!
>
> Thank you.
>
> Warm regards,
> Kachina

Kachina routinely consulted with the implementing team, particularly when they were unsure about the next steps in unfamiliar territory. She modeled the approach by asking the difficult questions. For example, regarding an initial fear or reluctance to bring TB Champions and health care providers together in the same room, she spoke the unspoken.

> "I sense a hesitation and I am going to call it. The beauty of this methodology is talking between stakeholders, not just within a

group of stakeholders. It's not all REACH team talking to the REACH team, or the leadership group talking to leadership, or TB Champions talking to TB Champions. It's about TB Champions having that engagement with other people. The beauty of the process is in its dialogue. How are you hoping to push that dialogue piece out."

Engaged Leadership

She also stayed in the game, participating in biweekly meetings, politely asking about progress, diplomatically asking about detours, and suggesting novel ways to rethink existing strategies in light of COVID and political obstacles. She was not deterred by problematic personalities or the relentless fear of the unknown. Kachina and Amrita were engaged leaders from USAID, who helped to create an honest, constructive learning climate and an evaluation transformation that facilitated social change.

> Kachina and Amrita were engaged leaders from USAID, who helped to create an honest, constructive learning climate and an evaluation transformation designed to facilitate social change.

Enlisted Support

They also recognized the need to enlist the help of a support team to facilitate the empowerment evaluation remotely. They recruited Subrat Mohanty, a leader of the REACH program implementation and evaluation agency, as noted earlier. He provided much of the organizational support required to sustain the long-term endeavor, including recruiting Rahul Dutta, the "key" program manager and evaluator, and his colleague at REACH, Valencia Souza. Both leaders operated on the national, state, and local levels.

USAID sponsors also helped to recruit the Catalyst group, the infrastructural support and technical assistance team, to help plan, execute, and record each step. Sandip Pattanayak, Catherine Cove, and Sabhimanvi Dua were instrumental in this regard, planning regular meetings, following up on critical tasks, and documenting deliberations and decisions. These donor agents of change even had the foresight to recruit additional colleagues in the field, including Drs. Jayalakshmi Shreedar and Sripriya Pandurangan, to help facilitate change in the health care system as part of this initiative.

Spread the Word

Catherine Cove and Shrirupa Sengupta created opportunities to increase exposure, in the form of webinars, articles, and social media interviews (see Figure 4.10).

Together these leaders and change agents had the vision of how empowerment evaluation could be used to help transform health care in India, with a focus on eliminating TB.

CONCLUSION

The example in Chapter 3 of Feeding America's fight for food justice in the United States (and the elimination of food insecurity) highlighted how empowerment evaluation is being integrated into existing evaluation frameworks and agreements. The USAID-funded initiative to eliminate TB demonstrates how empowerment evaluation was integrated into the preexisting workplan.

FIGURE 4.10. Shrirupa Sengupta interview with David Fetterman and Catherine Cove about empowerment evaluation on Swasti Café (*www.youtube.com/watch?v=IznfnqKI8vY*).

In both cases, the empowerment evaluations were not conducted in a vacuum. They were facilitated within the context of preexisting contractual agreements. However, in both cases the preexisting plans were reframed. They were made more meaningful because they were now housed within the local community and program staff members' view of what was needed to accomplish their goals.

5

Tech Tools

Conducting Empowerment Evaluation Remotely

> *The worldwide web of meaning is only what we make it mean.*

Tech tools and the Internet are responsible for the worldwide dissemination of empowerment evaluation (Fetterman, 2001). They have been invaluable for the application and facilitation of empowerment evaluation. However, online tools and the Internet are the most dreaded topics to document and discuss because they change as rapidly as you can write about them.

The Internet did not even exist when I wrote the first edition of one of my methods books, so there were no references to it. In the second edition, I made the mistake of using URLs, which changed almost immediately. By the third and fourth editions, I learned to use the name of the software and then the concept to make the discussion less likely to be dated in nanoseconds (see Fetterman, 1989, 1998, 2009b, and 2020). This is the approach adopted for this chapter.

> Tech tools and the Internet are responsible for the worldwide dissemination of empowerment evaluation.

The tech tools are organized into two categories: core tech tools and additional-support tech tools to facilitate empowerment evaluations. The use of core and additional-support tech tools overlap in practice. However, grouping them into these categories makes it easier to apply them appropriately.

CORE TOOLS

Empowerment evaluations can be conducted remotely with as little as two tools: videoconferencing software and an online spreadsheet. The remaining tech tools, although not critical, transform the quality and impact of an empowerment evaluation.

Videoconferencing Software

Videoconferencing enables people to see, hear, and speak with one another from a distance (see Figure 5.1). It creates a virtual space for personal contact and communication. At minimum it creates an approximation of face-to-face interaction. We use Zoom and Google Meet for our TB-elimination empowerment evaluation meetings, workshops, and facilitations. Webex Meeting is the preferred tool for Feeding America meetings and conferences. Additional videoconferencing platforms include Google Meet, Microsoft Teams, and Skype. VooV is often used for our communication with Chinese colleagues and clients because the use of other videoconferencing software is often prohibited in China.

Remotely conducted empowerment evaluations typically begin on Zoom, Webex Meeting, or Google Meet. Personal introductions are

FIGURE 5.1. Zoom videoconference with Angela Odoms-Young, encouraging food banks to apply a racial equity lens to their work and their empowerment evaluations.

followed by a brief overview of the approach. The whiteboard feature is used to illustrate ideas and formats. The annotation feature is used to highlight and illuminate a point in the discussion. The chat function is used for sidebar comments, clarification, and/or process questions, without disrupting the larger group's exchange. Most of our empowerment evaluation sessions (and many biweekly meetings) are recorded. As discussed in Chapter 6 (on frequently asked questions), having access to recordings helps people stay in the loop when they are unable to attend our synchronous sessions. In addition, the recordings create a historic record of the group's events, discussions, and agreements. Videoconferencing continues throughout the empowerment evaluation exercises; however, the group's focus and activity migrates to an online spreadsheet.

> Empowerment evaluations can be conducted remotely with as little as two tools: videoconferencing software and an online spreadsheet.

Online Spreadsheets

Google Sheets and Microsoft Excel are two of the most commonly used online spreadsheets. These online spreadsheets represent the tech heart and soul of a three-step empowerment evaluation. We use Google Sheets for our USAID-funded work in India and our U.S.-based work with Feeding America. Microsoft Excel has been useful for other empowerment evaluation projects in the United States, including our work with minority architectural firms. Google Sheets is best suited for collaboration and chatting functions. Microsoft Excel is superior for statistical analysis and for managing a higher volume of data.

We invite stakeholders to their designated spreadsheet a few days before the initial exercise. This helps to maximize the group's time on task by reducing downtime needed to respond to technical issues during the three-step exercise. Eliminating distractions also helps to maintain the focus and momentum of the group.

> Online spreadsheets represent the tech heart and soul of a three-step empowerment evaluation.

Mission

The REACH staff in India and the food bank grantees in the United States are asked to type their thoughts about their Mission on the first page of their respective spreadsheets. They are reminded to find a "clear" cell on the spreadsheet, so that they do not type over anyone else's comments. The ideas generated during the first step of the empowerment

> The ideas generated during the first step of the empowerment evaluation exercise provide the group with a common vision of what the group wants and where the group is going. The exercise is also a form of mental scaffolding, preparing the group for self-assessment or Taking Stock.

evaluation exercise provide the group with a common vision of what the group wants and where the group is going. The exercise is also a form of mental scaffolding, preparing the group for self-assessment or Taking Stock. (The comments of group members are woven into a Mission statement at a later date so as not to interfere with the flow of their conversation and interaction. They share the draft Mission statements using Google Docs [a collaborative word-processing online program] in order to reach a consensus about the Mission [see Figure 5.2].)

Taking Stock (Prioritization)

A new page labeled Taking Stock (prioritization) is created on the same spreadsheet as the Mission page (see Figure 5.3). Feeding America's Starbucks' grantees and USAID-funded project stakeholders in India

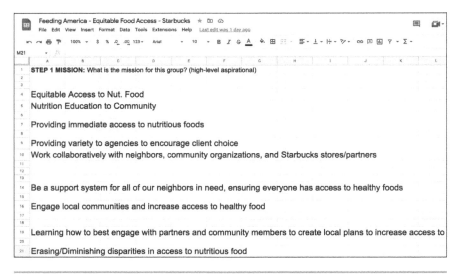

FIGURE 5.2. Feeding America empowerment evaluation Mission using Google Sheets.

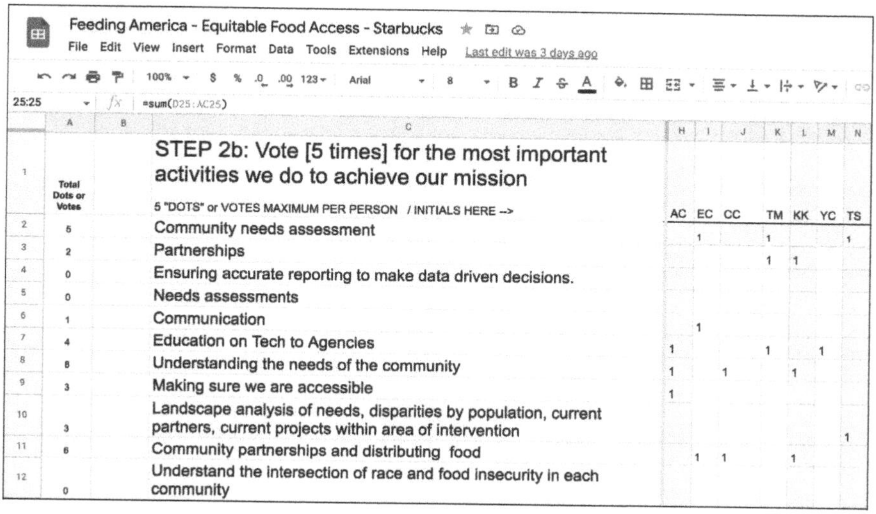

	Total Dots or Votes	STEP 2b: Vote [5 times] for the most important activities we do to achieve our mission 5 "DOTS" or VOTES MAXIMUM PER PERSON / INITIALS HERE -->	AC	EC	CC	TM	KK	YC	TS
2	6	Community needs assessment		1		1			1
3	2	Partnerships				1	1		
4	0	Ensuring accurate reporting to make data driven decisions.							
5	0	Needs assessments							
6	1	Communication		1					
7	4	Education on Tech to Agencies	1			1		1	
8	8	Understanding the needs of the community	1		1		1		
9	3	Making sure we are accessible	1						
10	3	Landscape analysis of needs, disparities by population, current partners, current projects within area of intervention							1
11	6	Community partnerships and distributing food		1	1		1		
12	0	Understand the intersection of race and food insecurity in each community							

FIGURE 5.3. Feeding America Taking Stock (Prioritization).

generate a list of the most important activities they are engaged in to make the Mission possible. Additional columns are created. The stakeholders place their initials at the tops of these columns and place their "votes" in the columns under their initials. Their votes are used to determine what they think are the most important activities to rate and discuss as a group.

Each stakeholder gets five votes. The number of votes are totaled at the bottom of each column to ensure that everyone only voted five times. In addition the votes are totaled horizontally for each individual by activity. The top 10 activities with the most votes are transferred to the next page labeled Taking Stock (rating and dialogue).

The Taking Stock ratings page resembles a typical spreadsheet. One column consists of a list of the top 10 activities, or the activities that received the most votes in the Taking Stock prioritization exercise. The remaining columns capture each person's ratings of the activities. Each individual's initials are recorded at the top of the columns. The ratings for each program activity are recorded in each individual's column, using a 1 (low) to 10 (high) scale.

Similar to the Taking Stock prioritization page, the ratings on the Taking Stock rating and dialogue page are totaled, and in this case an average is calculated horizontally across individuals by activity (see

Feeding America - Equitable Food Access - Starbucks

File Edit View Insert Format Data Tools Extensions Help Last edit was 3 days ago

	AVG Rating	STEP 2c: How well are we doing on each one of these prioritized activities? Scale: 1=Terrible and 10 = Perfect (Initials here ->)	DF	EK	CC	AC	TM	EC	YC	TS	LK	DP	HG	NA	MR	TMc	LH	LB
2	7.87	Increased distribution of nutritious food		8	8	10	9	8	6	8	7	8	10	9	6	7	7	7
3	6.33	Understanding the needs of the community		6	7	6	8	6	4	10	7	5	8	7	4	6	5	6
4	6.93	Improving operations and systems to better serve those in need		8	5	7	8	7	9	8	6	6	7	6	7	7	6	7
5	7.29	Community partnerships and distributing food			7	8	8	7	5	7	7	8	7	6	8	7	9	8
6	5.27	Gather community input		5	4	5	8	4	6	7	6	2	7	6	5	4	5	5
7	5.53	make sure all employees, agencies, and funders are aligned in mission and efforts		5	5	5	6	4	1	8	8	1	9	8	5	5	6	7
8	5.20	Identify access barriers and determine solutions		7	6	7	2	5	3	7	5	2	6	4	6	6	6	6
9	4.73	Community needs assessment		5	7	5	2	5	8	4	4	1	7	4	5	5	4	5

FIGURE 5.4. Taking Stock (Rating and Dialogue).

Figure 5.4). This calculation produces a portrait of both individual ratings concerning each prioritized activity and the group's combined and averaged ratings concerning each of the activities. A graph of the group's ratings can be generated on the same page to help individual members look at their self-assessments, similar to seeing their assessments through a digital lens.

> A graph of the group's assessment of each activity creates a baseline document, which can be compared with future Taking Stock (rating and dialogue) exercises.

This record of the group's assessment of each activity creates a baseline document that can be compared with future Taking Stock (rating and dialogue) exercises. It also sets the stage for one of the most important parts of this Taking Stock exercise: dialogue.

Taking Stock (Dialogue)

The groups continue to communicate online with Zoom or a similar videoconferencing platform. However, the same Taking Stock (rating) spreadsheet is used as a focal point and launching pad for the next phase—unpacking the ratings and dialogue. The facilitator uses individuals' initials to identify members of the group in order to ask them for their reasons or evidence for their ratings.

The Feeding America and USAID-funded project conversations have been robust, approximating the same level of engagement found in most face-to-face gatherings. The elephant in the room emerged in both of these empowerment evaluations, as noted earlier. One focused on the fear of moving forward in bringing potentially adversarial groups together. The second was focused on defining terms, as discussed in Chapter 3, such as food security and food justice. The third issue involved questioning the relevance of preexisting survey questions. In addition, both groups recorded the conversations, which enabled them to mine them for insights and patterns in the future. The shared evidence that explained the rationale for the ratings was also used to construct strategies in the Planning for the Future step.

Evaluative Core

Stakeholders in the U.S. and Indian empowerment evaluations reflected on their respective individual average ratings. The ratings highlighted who was optimistic and who was pessimistic on average, which helped them assess all future ratings by their colleagues. For example, one of the stakeholder's ratings on average was 3.5 concerning most of the listed activities. We took notice when she rated an activity a 5 or a 6 because we knew she was normally more critical than most of the members of the group.

> Comparing stakeholder ratings helped group members get to know one another from their evaluative core, as compared with their political, religious, and cultural core.

Comparing stakeholder ratings helped group members get to know one another from their evaluative core, as compared with their political, religious, and cultural core. Once many of the critical issues were examined and discussed, the groups were ready to enter the next phase: Planning for the Future.

Planning for the Future

The TB elimination teams and the Feeding America food bank grantees created their Plans for the Future on the next page of their spreadsheets (see Figure 5.5) and included three of the Taking Stock activities. The Plans for the Future also included three topics: goals, strategies, and evidence. The stakeholders wrote their goals, the strategies for achieving the goals, and the evidence that the strategies were implemented for the

Feeding America - Equitable Food Access - Starbucks ⭐
File Edit View Insert Format Data Tools Extensions Help · Last edit was 2 minutes ago

A1 | Capital Area Food Bank

	A	B
1	**Capital Area Food Bank**	
2		
3	Type Your Name	
4	Type Your Email	
5		
6	**Goal**	Better understand our clients accessing our existing Community Marketplaces in Reston, VA and Washington, DC to ensure that our program is thoughtfully addressing food access barriers in BIPOC communities in Fairfax, VA and Washington, DC and including client voice in decision-making.
7		Engage our Starbucks Community Store team members in CAFB distributions in their community
8		
9	**Strategies**	Review and analyze Link2Feed data to better understand where clients live and how far they travel to the Community Marketplace
10		Survey clients to better understand their needs in terms of desired food items, day/time of distributions, community resources desired to invite to have onsite during Markets. Include client voices in discussions about adjustments to Marketplaces.
11		Examine our Hunger Heat Map and in conjunction with L2F data and client surveys, examine ideal locations for existing distributions to ensure that we are providing culturally familiar food items equitably across our region. Work with both community and CAFB Partners to identify any new Marketplace locations and engage clients in any transition planning.
12		
13		
14		
15	**Evidence**	Work with our Analytics team to build L2F Dashboards that capture Community Marketplaces client demographics (and those who have not re-engaged with the Market) - FY22 Q3
16		Work with our Analytics team to build pulse surveys to implement at Community Marketplaces (FY22 late Q3/early Q4) - # of surveys completed
17		Dedicate funds (unsure of $) to purchase culturally familiar foods and produce fresh produce from local BIPOC growers. - % of food items CF and locally sourced from BIPOC growers

FIGURE 5.5. Feeding America Planning for the Future.

three activities. This step represented the groups' intervention or strategic plan.

This online spreadsheet was used to document the three-step process and prepared each group to construct evaluation dashboards. The evaluation dashboards were placed on the remaining pages of the spreadsheet.

> The Plans for the Future included three topics: goals, strategies, and evidence.

Evaluation Dashboards

Feeding America/Starbucks grantees and USAID/REACH colleagues created evaluation dashboards to monitor their ongoing progress. They consisted of tables with the following information: baseline, goals, milestones, and actual performance (see Figure 5.6). Bar graphs were created in order to help community and staff members monitor their own performance over time (see Figure 5.7). They were also used to visually inform administrators, donors, and outside parties about the group's progress.

> Evaluation dashboards have baselines, goals, milestones, and actual performance.

Additional Notes

The spreadsheets were reused in future empowerment evaluation exercises. Participants removed the data and made a copies of the empty spreadsheets with the formulas intact. Computer screen snapshots were also taken at each step in the process to record the group's engagement. These Taking Stock graphs and computer screen snapshots were used in various reports to document the group's process and productivity.

Identify Key Members & Partners

	Q1	Q2	Q3	Q4
Actual Performance	0	0		
Milestones	2	3	5	7
Goal	7	7	7	7

FIGURE 5.6. Evaluation dashboard table.

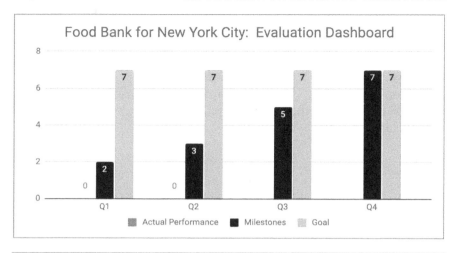

FIGURE 5.7. Evaluation dashboard graph.

ADDITIONAL SUPPORT TOOLS

Many other tech tools are used to support empowerment evaluations. Qualitative data and statistical analysis software are routinely selected to determine if Plans for the Future are being implemented and are having an impact. Examples of qualitative data analysis packages include NVivo, ATLAS/ti, and HyperRESEARCH. A couple of the most common quantitative software packages are SPSS Statistics and SAS. They are discussed in depth in most research courses and methods textbooks (Delwiche & Slaughter, 2019; Fetterman, 2020; Field, 2017; Jackson & Bazeley, 2021; Saldana, 2021; Salkind & Frey, 2019).

This chapter highlights additional tech tools that commonly support empowerment evaluations, but are less commonly discussed in textbooks. They range from alternative avatar-based meeting software to powerful data visualization and presentation tools, with an assortment of tech tools in between.

Scheduling

Scheduling is considered one of the most mundane activities in our busy lives but is an absolute necessity, particularly when juggling multiple projects and multiple teams. In addition to adding to our efficiency, scheduling sends a symbolic message. Lateness, missing meetings, unresponsiveness or tardiness concerning requests for meetings, and failure to invite all the appropriate people to a meeting all send a message of arrogance, irresponsibility, exclusivity, or, at minimum, unprofessional behavior. Scheduling meetings, inviting all relevant parties, and attending meetings demonstrate both professionalism and a person's respect for people's time and contributions. Feeding America and USAID colleagues use Google Calendar and Microsoft Outlook, two of the most common calendaring tools, to plan empowerment evaluation exercises and to remind stakeholders of timelines and deadlines.

The reminder feature in their calendaring software alerts users about upcoming meetings. In addition, these tools allow community and staff members to share their calendars with other members in the community and the evaluation team. The calendaring software also automatically adjusts for time zone differences. For example, Google Calendar automatically kept my USAID-funded TB elimination biweekly meetings in India on track with my U.S. schedule, when it was 8:30 A.M. in New Delhi and 11:00 P.M. the day before in the United States (see Figure 5.8). Similarly, Google Calendar accounted for different time zones in the United States, helping me coordinate schedules with my

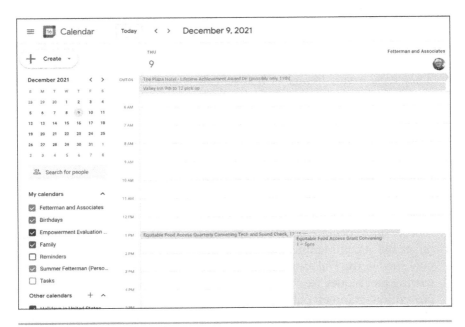

FIGURE 5.8. Google Calendar.

food security/food justice, tobacco prevention, and addiction studies empowerment evaluations in Arkansas and Illinois. Additional scheduling tools used to determine a mutually convenient time to meet include Calendar, Calendly, Doodle, Rally, and Need-ToMeet. These online calendaring tools minimized common scheduling errors. In the process, these tools built trust and good will while helping to get things done.

> Simple shared calendars build trust and good will by demonstrating a respect for other people's time.

Training Tools

Empowerment evaluation is focused on capacity building. We provide on-demand training in mini-modules throughout the empowerment evaluations, particularly after stakeholders have completed the Planning for the Future step. This step represents the group's intervention, and it is the stage at which the group needs additional evaluation tools to monitor and assess its progress and outcomes.

Typical training sessions provided in our tobacco prevention in minority communities' empowerment evaluations and in our TB elimination efforts in India have included training in interviewing, observation, online survey software, videoconferencing software, descriptive statistics, and reporting of findings. YouTube and Vimeo are widely recognized capacity-building tech tools. They have a vast library of how-to videos and instructional materials. Simple empowerment evaluation training modules can be accessed at the YouTube library at no additional expense (see Figure 5.9).

> Empowerment evaluation is focused on capacity building.

Additional tech tools have been used to help community and evaluation team members learn about evaluation. They are short how-to modules demonstrating specific evaluation tools and techniques. For example, Loom can be used to record a brief explanation about how to write op-eds. Specifically, I used Loom to record an op-ed I wrote about banning menthol-flavored tobacco products. It was related to my tobacco-prevention empowerment evaluation since tobacco companies target Black communities with these products. I shared my op-ed pieces, published in the *Philadelphia Inquirer* and *The Mercury News*, to highlight writing techniques (see Figure 5.10). I also recommended that tobacco-prevention grantees publish similar tobacco prevention and cessation articles in their local newspapers. Key elements of the op-ed were visually highlighted in the foreground on my computer screen. Simultaneously, I

FIGURE 5.9. YouTube video of David Fetterman's Ignite Lecture.

The Mercury News

Commentary | Why U.S. should ban menthol flavored tobacco...

OPINION COMMENTARY · News, Opinion

Why U.S. should ban menthol flavored tobacco products

Smoking kills more people than alcohol, AIDS, car crashes, illegal drugs, murders and suicides combined

A small sampling of tobacco and vaping products, including the popular Juul brand vape and mango flavored cartridges of e-liquid for it, are seen on a table at a meeting about tobacco availability in Fremont on Nov. 15, 2018. Fremont banned sales of all flavored tobacco in 2018. (Joseph Geha/Bay Area News Group)

By DAVID FETTERMAN |
PUBLISHED: April 12, 2022 at 5:15 a.m. | UPDATED: April 12, 2022 at 5:25 a.m.

FIGURE 5.10. Op-ed about banning menthol-flavored tobacco (*The Mercury News*).

described how pieces of the op-ed were constructed and designed to have a specific effect. Similarly, Loom enabled me to demonstrate to group members how to use software programs on their computers. The instructional videos were viewed by large numbers of people asynchronously and on their own schedules, saving the instructors time and providing people with the flexibility to view the videos whenever they found it convenient.

Meeting

Zoom and other videoconferencing software are invaluable contributions for teaching, researching, evaluating, and maintaining family and social relationships. However, alternatives are needed since Zoom fatigue and other attention-diminishing factors associated with online learning have been well documented.

Alternatives that complement traditional videoconference meetings and exchanges exist. One of the more popular avatar-based meeting software programs is Virbela (see Figure 5.11). It allows the user to create her

FIGURE 5.11. Virbela (Linda Delaney and David Fetterman preparing for a tobacco-prevention empowerment evaluation workshop).

or his own avatar and select skin and hair color, clothing, shoes, and glasses. The avatars meet in virtual rooms, auditoriums, and even at beaches. They speak through their computer microphones in private or in groups. They can present their PowerPoint slides inside a virtual meeting or classroom. Linda Delaney and I prepared one of our tobacco-prevention empowerment evaluation planning meetings using this platform. An avatar-based meeting platform provides a refreshing and more embodied alternative to the standard format of online communication and meetings.

> An avatar-based meeting platform provides a refreshing and more embodied alternative to the standard format of online communication and meetings.

MURAL

MURAL is a visual online collaboration tool (see Figure 5.12) for brainstorming, diagramming, voting, and facilitating online celebrations. It is like Google Sheets on steroids because it is more visually appealing. It can be used to facilitate three-step empowerment evaluations, including generating ideas to create or refine the Mission, brainstorming a list of the most important activities in the program, voting for the most important activities to rate and discuss, rating how well the group is conducting program activities from 1 (low) to 10 (high), and creating Plans for the Future. We have used the program for

> MURAL is like Google Sheets on steroids because it is more visually appealing.

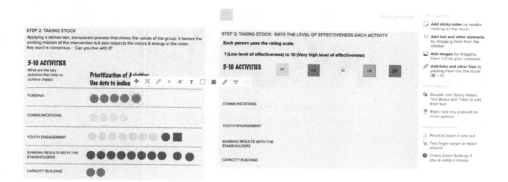

FIGURE 5.12. MURAL.

planning meetings and webinars and as a replacement for Google Sheets to change things up.

Google Forms

Google Forms is a free online survey software (see Figure 5.13) that enables community and staff members (with the assistance of a critical friend) to survey community members about a problem, a new initiative, or a particular demographic, or satisfaction with current program activities and initiatives. It is typically used after the Plans for the Future are completed and evaluation dashboards are constructed. Google Forms is easy to work with, and the data can be downloaded into Excel for additional analysis. The software helped us in our tobacco-prevention empowerment evaluations to determine how much statewide support there was for the program. The Feeding America grantees used a similar online survey software to determine if their neighbors or clients were able to access food in their neighborhoods without confronting racial discrimination and related indignities.

> Google Forms is a free online survey software.

Google's Geographical Map Chart

The Geographical Map Chart is a free Google application derived from Google Sheets that enables community and staff members to visually

FIGURE 5.13. Online survey—Google Forms.

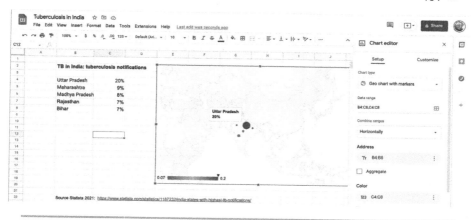

FIGURE 5.14. Geographical Map Chart.

map out the frequency of occurrences, the scale of a problem, and community assets by geographical location (see Figure 5.14). My colleagues are using geographical map charts to visually map out the frequency of TB by geographical location in the USAID/REACH TB-elimination empowerment evaluation in India and to help develop a plan of attack against the disease. A visual display also helped them prioritize TB prevention initiatives and rights-based training activities to make the health care system more sensitive to TB survivors' rights. They plan to compare these geographical maps over time to monitor progress in reducing TB in cities or regions and track rights-based training throughout India. (Geographical Map Chart instructions are available on Google or at AEA 365.)

> Geographical Map Chart enables community and staff members to visually map out the frequency of occurrences, the scale of a problem, and community assets by geographical location.

Canva

Canva is a graphic design platform that is used to create social media graphics, presentations, posters, and reports (see Figure 5.15). It raises the bar in terms of professional polish and presentation. We have provided Canva demonstrations and encouraged community and staff members to use it to prepare presentations, write proposals, draft evaluation reports, and post social media notices. The platform has been used in all of our empowerment evaluations, ranging from helping to draft empowerment

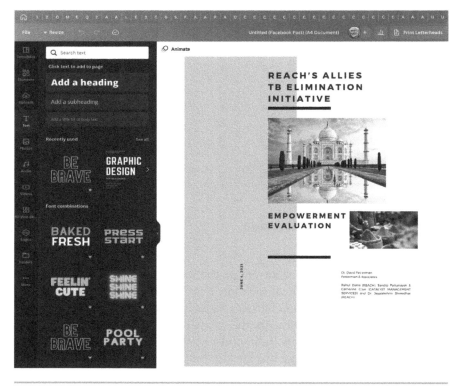

FIGURE 5.15. Canva (graphic design).

evaluation reports (summarizing the three-step approach and evaluation dashboard progress) to posting program highlights on social media.

Canva can also be used to create music video reports. These are graphically illustrated text reports with accompanying music. The PowerPoint-like pages automatically flip from page to page, like pages in a book, with music playing in the background. The upscale quality of the presentation entices donors and collaborating community agencies to read grantee progress reports and support their efforts.

Canva is easy to work with and does not require the same learning curve as other professional graphic design programs like Illustrator and CorelDRAW. Community agencies and donors view community-evaluation findings with greater respect and deference when they are "dressed up" in a professional package.

> Community agencies and donors view community-evaluation findings with greater respect and deference when they are "dressed up" in a professional package.

(See Evergreen, 2017, 2018, for illustrations of data visualization in evaluation.)

Social Media

LinkedIn (see Figure 5.16), Facebook, and Twitter are a few of the most frequently used social media platforms for posting empowerment evaluation activities, findings, and recommendations. Sharing Taking Stock activities, progress reports, and Plans for the Future on social media platforms gives programs greater visibility. Feeding America food bank grantees and stakeholders in India have posted on social media to keep the larger public informed about their activities and progress toward community-driven goals. They have also used postings for advocacy, highlighting program accomplishments in order to secure additional funding.

Social media postings create an invisible, but powerful network. For example, Native Americans have posted their empowerment evaluation activities on social media, including building one of the largest unlicensed wireless systems in the country (Fetterman, 2013a). First Nation tribes in Canada have used this infor-

> Social media postings create an invisible, but powerful network.

mation to advance their own successful ventures without any other intermediary. Social media has also been used in empowerment evaluations to crowdsource solutions to common community challenges and problems.

Cloud Storage

Google Drive, Google Photos, Dropbox, and Apple cloud storage platforms can be used to store and exchange large documents and pictures. The space is protected, and permission is required to access stored documents. However, once permission is obtained, this space facilitates collaborative work by making these docu-

> Cloud storage facilitates collaborative work by making the documents accessible from remote locations.

ments accessible from remote locations. All of our empowerment evaluation projects rely on cloud storage for archival purposes, file sharing, and remote accessibility. Similarly, our Feeding America food bank grantees rely on it to access survey documents and videos of our evaluation exercises, as well as PowerPoint presentations shared at our meetings throughout the empowerment evaluation.

FIGURE 5.16. LinkedIn (social media).

■ 104

Blogs

Blogger is a free blogging platform (see Figure 5.17). It provides community and staff members with the opportunity to publicly highlight their ongoing work and invite collaboration from programs that have similar interests and initiatives. It is as easy to use as most word processing programs. Blogging has a reputation for being self-indulgent and for reporting on the minutia of an individual's daily life with belly-gazing introspection. Community members and empowerment evaluators, however, are encouraged to use blogs to highlight their programs' accomplishments. The result is a professional-appearing web presence for the community and/or program.

Community members and empowerment evaluators are encouraged to use blogs to highlight their programs' accomplishments.

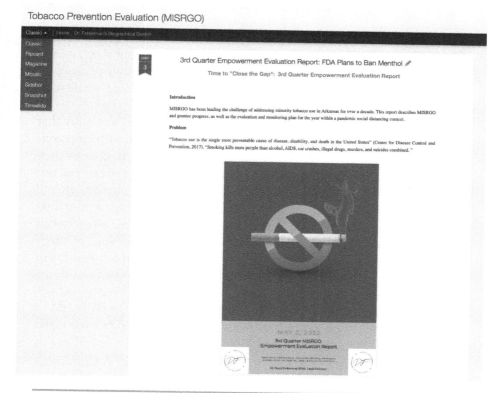

FIGURE 5.17. Blog.

Google Sites

Google Sites is a collaborative webpage. It enables community and staff members to create their own webpages and link them to a central hub or webpage to invite participation and collaboration. The Arkansas tobacco-prevention empowerment evaluation grantees used Google Sites to track each other's progress and to highlight the group's progress and accomplishments. These collaborative websites can also be used to advocate for additional resources.

> Google sites invites participation and collaboration.

CONCLUSION

Videoconferencing and online spreadsheet software programs represent the core tech tools of empowerment evaluations. There are, however, an almost infinite number of additional useful tech tools that support the facilitation of empowerment evaluations. The rule of thumb when selecting these tools is that they be user-friendly, free or inexpensive, and philosophically aligned with empowerment evaluation principles.

> The rule of thumb when selecting tech tools is that they be user-friendly, free or inexpensive, and philosophically aligned with empowerment evaluation principles.

For example, software that is so complex and difficult to modify that it discourages people from making changes is not aligned with empowerment evaluation principles. Participants need to be able to change their ratings after listening to their colleagues and friends present evidence for their ratings in an empowerment evaluation. The software should not inhibit or discourage them from changing their rating, during Taking Stock for example, simply because the software made the changes time-consuming and technically difficult to do. Similarly, purchasing prohibitively expensive software or software requiring a significant learning curve is discouraged, unless it is absolutely necessary to do so. Tech tools should be easily accessible (including from a cost perspective). These tools are neither good nor bad per se. They are simply useful or not useful. Judiciously used, they can amplify a community's voice and exponentially expand a community's impact.

6

Empowerment Evaluation

Frequently Asked Questions

Inquiry is the doorway to perception,
understanding, and action

Empowerment evaluation has a strong theoretical foundation, ranging from empowerment theory to process use. In addition, empowerment evaluation is grounded in practice. Hard-headed social justice examples can be found stretching across globe from one end to the other. Case examples range from schools to hospitals to government agencies to nonprofits and corporations. There is a long list of books, articles, videos, webinars, classes, and talks available to guide an empowerment evaluation in practice. Many colleagues learn how to facilitate an empowerment evaluation by complementing their immersion into the literature and lectures with experiential opportunities, including participating in empowerment evaluation exercises and conducting an empowerment evaluation with a seasoned empowerment evaluator.

> There is a long list of books, articles, videos, webinars, classes, and talks available to guide an empowerment evaluation in practice.

In spite of this wealth of knowledge and experiential opportunities, inevitably a host of pertinent questions arise. This is natural and expected. Applying the approach in practice should raise questions, requiring innovations and adaptations. Colleagues new to empowerment evaluation may find it radically different from conventional evaluations, particularly because the control of the evaluation is in the community's and staff members' hands. They have questions about objectivity and subjectivity, credibility, roles, and funders. Seasoned empowerment evaluators have more nuanced questions that arise from facilitating an empowerment evaluation. They range from questions about facilitation skills and integration strategies to questions about dissemination and advocacy. In addition, there are many logistical questions that arise as colleagues and community members apply the approach. Many of these questions are addressed in the existing literature (Fetterman, 2001, 2013a, 2015c, 2017, 2018; Fetterman et al., 2010; Fetterman, Kaftarian, et al., 2015; Fetterman et al., 2018; Fetterman & Wandersman, 2005, 2017).

Nevertheless, some of the most common questions that surface from students, workshop participants, community empowerment evaluators, and interested colleagues are addressed in this chapter to further guide good practice. The questions are organized into the following categories: Big Picture (Conceptual, Theoretical, and Philosophical); Mind Bending or Counterintuitive; Community Control; Fear of Losing Control; Multiple Perspectives; Methodological; Practical; and Mechanical.

BIG PICTURE (CONCEPTUAL, THEORETICAL, AND PHILOSOPHICAL)

Q. Is empowerment evaluation used for learning or for accountability?

A. Both. Empowerment evaluation is focused on learning. Programs develop and mature over time. The community context is dynamic, not static. Many new programs are just our best guess at what's needed. Therefore, it is imperative that we use evaluation to learn, grow, adapt, and build on knowledge.

Empowerment evaluation also asks the question: did you do it? It is aimed at producing desired outcomes or results. Empowerment evaluation does not stop at the Taking Stock step of rating and dialogue. It asks people to state where they want to go next in the Plans for the Future step. In addition, empowerment evaluation uses evaluation dashboards for accountability purposes. Evaluation dashboards are designed to help community members, grantees, and staff members monitor their performance and make midcourse corrections in order to accomplish their goals. Outcomes matter.

> Empowerment evaluations are used for both learning and accountability.

Q. What do you do if there is a preexisting evaluation and/or work-plan in place?

A. You use empowerment evaluation to ground the existing evaluation and workplan in a community context and perception of what's needed. Empowerment evaluations do not exist in a vacuum. There is always a larger context.

Empowerment evaluations are typically conducted within the context of what people are already being held accountable for in their own world. The superintendent of a school district has a directive and plan to reduce the dropout rate. Teachers and nurses use empowerment evaluation to determine how they can contribute to those objectives. Prime ministers make commitments to improving health by advocating for specific programs aimed at eliminating TB and reducing HIV rates. Their health care providers and community activists use empowerment evaluation to determine what they can do to assist in achieving those larger national, state, and community goals.

> Empowerment evaluations are typically conducted within the context of what people are already being held accountable for in their own world.

Similarly, many nonprofit, faith-based health organizations are committed (and contracted) to preventing tobacco consumption or stopping smoking in minority communities. Community and staff members use empowerment evaluation to determine if they are accomplishing their objectives.

Frequently, there are preexisting evaluation designs and workplans in place. Chapters 3 and 4 provide examples of how to integrate empowerment evaluation into these types of preexisting evaluation designs and workplans.

Q. Can you use empowerment evaluation to advocate for a program? Doesn't advocacy contradict or undermine the integrity or objectivity of an evaluation?

A. Yes. You can use empowerment evaluation to advocate for a program if the data merit it. People have always used evaluation to advocate for a program. This is nothing new. The difference is that empowerment evaluation typically highlights what's working to address what's not working (and to solicit funds to address those problems).

Empowerment evaluation highlights what people think they are doing well, with credible evidence. This approach places them in an excellent position to inform a sponsor or donor about what they are not doing well and need help to address. They can document an exemplary track record of accomplishing their objectives with sufficient support and thus can be trusted as a reliable group to address areas meriting attention (with additional support). If everything is going perfectly, why would anyone need additional support?

> You can use empowerment evaluation to advocate for a program if the data merit it.

Q. Can empowerment evaluation be used for liberation?

A. Yes. There are two streams of empowerment discussed in Chapter 1. One is practical and focuses on practical problems. Transformative empowerment evaluation is a second stream, and it is concerned with the psychological, social, and political power of liberation. It focuses on liberation from prescribed conventional roles and "ways of doing things."

It has been used in townships in South Africa to raise consciousness, transform relationships, and address a broad range of community-participation health care programs. It has also been used to help nurses in public school districts redefine their roles and responsibilities as health care providers for our children (Fetterman, 2001).

> Transformative empowerment evaluation is concerned with the psychological, social, and political power of liberation.

Empowerment evaluation has also been used to help liberate evaluators from their constraining and limited roles as experts who foster dependency instead of capacity builders contributing to self-determination and sustainability.

Q. Who benefits from an empowerment evaluation approach?

A. We all do. The community member who has been given a voice and is taking charge of his or her life benefits from empowerment evaluation. Staff members have a better idea about what's working in their programs from their client's perspective. Administrators are more in touch with their own programs. Donors see a return on their investment in terms of capacity building and sustainability as well as in better outcomes. The public benefits because empowerment evaluation helps people improve outcomes.

> We all benefit from an empowerment evaluation approach.

MIND BENDING OR COUNTERINTUITIVE

Q. What is the secret to empowerment evaluation? Why does it work?

A. Self-interest: either mutual self-interest or common denominators of self-interest. I was told I would fail when I began working on an empowerment evaluation in a community comprising Blacks, Latinx, and Pacific Islanders, and a variety of additional racial and ethnic groups with a lot of cultural baggage, a history of competition for the same resources, and a great deal of distrust. I asked people to raise their hands if they were willing to work on improving schools for their kids. Hands went up across the board, regardless of racial or ethnic background. The same question applied to improving security in the community. We could not agree on housing, so we only worked on education and security issues. The key to empowerment evaluation's success is that everyone is asked to put their self-interest on the table and then identify the common denominators of self-interest. Everyone needs to advocate for themselves and put some skin in the game.

> Mutual self-interest or common denominators of self-interest are the secret of the success of empowerment evaluation.

Q. You have said you should be as inefficient as possible. What do you mean by that?

A. I have made the mistake of being too efficient. For example, I have asked medical administrators to go off and come up with Plans for the Future on their own to save time. When the administrators returned, no one could agree with anyone about anything. It was smarter to sit down, take some time, and come to a consensus about what we wanted to do together in the Plans for the Future step instead of trying to be efficient and sending everyone away before we had a sense of where we wanted to go in common first. It is better to be inefficient (and take the time to get on the same page) than it is to be efficient (initially), only to have to revisit (and sometime retrofit) the same plans and strategies over and over again.

> It is better to take the time to get on the same page than to have to revisit the same plans and strategies over and over again.

Q. What do you mean when you say you want people to be biased or influenced by each other's viewpoints?

A. I have found it invaluable for folks to know what other community and staff members are thinking about and prioritizing during the first part of Taking Stock (when each person uses dot stickers to select activities). They should see where the energy in the room is going so they don't waste their vote (or dilute their input) on activities no one is selecting at that time.

However, I typically ask community and staff members to record their ratings on a separate piece of paper before recording their ratings on

> In empowerment evaluation, it is invaluable for folks to know what other community and staff members are thinking about.

the poster paper in the second part of Taking Stock (rating and dialogue). This task creates some independence for the members before they see where they stand in relation to others in the group and also allows them to see whether they are aligned with the larger group or are outliers. This is the point at which the engagement is at its height and dialogue is the most rewarding. It is periodically conflictual, but dependably generative and insightful.

It is also important for members to see one another's ratings and listen to their rationale for their ratings during the second part of Taking Stock. There is no hiding behind a rating in the comfort of traditional confidentiality and anonymity. People may agree or disagree with the ratings and/or evidence but the information is out in the open for all to consider, defend, and grapple with.

Q. What do you mean when you say we have all been socialized the wrong way?

A. As evaluators we have been socialized to be in complete control. We are the experts. We rarely concern ourselves with leaving something behind. We need to let go and allow community and staff members to take control over their own lives. We also need to help them develop their evaluation capacity by being in charge of the evaluation and conducting it as a group. But we do not abdicate our responsibility. We remain in the group to assist them as critical friends, knowing that they need to be in charge of the goals and strategies, as well as the ratings and dialogue.

Community and staff member also need to rethink evaluation. At first, they are enthusiastic about taking charge of an evaluation. However, once deadlines surface and budget concerns reemerge, they are all too happy to return to traditional roles, asking the evaluator to take control of conducting the evaluation. This is where the evaluator has to stand strong and say, "No, we are going to do it together."

Finally, we all have to rethink and reconceptualize the role of the funder. Most of us see the funder as the agency bankrolling the project or initiative. We want funders to drop the funds off and disappear. However, if we think about funders this way, we are missing an important opportunity. Their wealth is not just in dollars, it is in the knowledge they possess about the various social programs they invest in. We should be tapping them for their knowledge, not just for what's in their wallets.

Q. What do you mean when you say, do less to do more?

A. The entire empowerment evaluation process is designed to create a concentrated "dose effect." It is a process of reduction. The group begins with the largest possible starting point—the Mission. It is not possible to do everything in life or in an evaluation. The prioritization part of Taking Stock aims to reduce the focus from the large-scale, long-range mission to the most important activities to assess by the group at a given time. The group takes a deep dive and discusses some of the key activities in greater depth during the dialogue phase of the Taking Stock step. Finally, the group selects the top three activities from the Taking Stock step and creates three highly focused Plans for the Future. This approach helps people do more by focusing on fewer highly prioritized and discussed activities.

> The entire empowerment evaluation process is designed to create a concentrated "dose effect."

Q. Why do you say the subjective viewpoint is as important as the objective viewpoint?

A. I worked at a Veterans Administration psychiatric hospital many years ago. Many of the men thought they could fly. You may not think they could fly. I might not think they could fly. However, there were real-world consequences for that perception of reality on the third floor of a psych ward with no bars on the window. The subjective perception of reality is as important as the objective perception because people's behavior is shaped and determined by their perception of reality.

> People's behavior is shaped and determined by their perception of reality.

Q. Isn't it natural for people to want to make themselves look good and say that everything is okay?

A. Not really. First, if you give people an opportunity to share what's working, they are more inclined to share what's not working. Moreover, most people do not want to live and work in a broken or dysfunctional environment day after day. Empowerment evaluation provides them with a window of opportunity to fix what's broken. People dedicated to improving their communities and programs are typically more critical than outside or external reviewers because they want the program to work.

> Empowerment evaluation provides people with a window of opportunity to fix what's broken.

Q. What do you mean, we try to work ourselves out of a job?

A. The aim of an empowerment evaluation is to have people conduct their evaluations themselves. They are in charge of the evaluation. However, we serve as coaches and critical friends to keep it on track, honest, and rigorous. I may conduct the first empowerment evaluation exercise with a member of the community. I typically follow up with another workshop or exercise, with the community member taking the lead however. I remain involved with the group as a colleague backing up the community member. Eventually, I only prepare the community leaders and debrief them, so that community members are looking to them, not to me, for leadership and guidance.

However, life is rarely linear and straightforward. People do not always follow through, some are fearful of change and backtrack, and others procrastinate. People also move away and leave the project and the community. These are all natural real-life circumstances and conditions. The empowerment evaluator often needs to jump in and pair the stronger members of the evaluation team with those needing assistance, provide additional training, find new partners when others drop out, and revisit temporarily resolved issues. Working oneself out of a job is much harder and more time-consuming than it appears at first glance, but it should remain the goal.

> The aim of an empowerment evaluation is to have people conduct their evaluations themselves.

Q. Is empowerment evaluation neutral?

A. No. It is not neutral. It aims to help people use evaluation feedback loops to accomplish their goals and to help them build capacity and foster self-determination.

No evaluation is neutral. The ideal of neutrality is an appealing illusion. The questions posed, the budget allocated, and the type of program selected are all reflections of bias, position, and interpretation.

Nevertheless, empowerment evaluation within this larger social and political context is methodologically honest, rigorous, and credible. It is also typically more critical than traditional evaluations because the empowerment evaluator, community members, and staff members want the program to succeed.

> Empowerment evaluation is honest, rigorous, and credible.

COMMUNITY CONTROL

Q. Why is ownership important in empowerment evaluation? Why don't you just give people surveys and other metrics?

A. I have conducted many evaluations of satellite pharmacies in hospitals. They are small, decentralized pharmacies located in specific departments in a hospital, such as pediatrics and oncology. I remember rushing into one of these satellite pharmacies and asking a colleague to complete a log I needed in preparation for a meeting with the administration about staffing and workload distributions. The pharmacist responded to my request in exasperation, "David, I am a working supervisor. I have these folks I have to monitor and look at the number of scrips I have to fill every morning." I said, "Sorry, I was just in too much of a rush. You tell me what we need to do to let them [the administration] know what kind of workload demands you have."

He grabbed a piece of blank paper from his counter, drew a few lines on it, and said, "If I wrote down how many pediatric prescriptions I fill in an hour, with a time and date column here on the right side. . . ." I did not interrupt him, but he was in effect suggesting a log. That is precisely what I had just asked him to complete, but now it was coming from him.

> When people complete the forms they created, they have a sense of ownership of the evaluation.

His data collection strategy (and instrument) responded to a need in his daily life. The log made sense because he created it, it was contextualized, and it fit into his frame of reference. Completing the log he made contributed to a sense of ownership of the evaluation, making data collection more meaningful and relevant. It also made the results credible.

Purpose should precede metrics.

FEAR OF LOSING CONTROL

Q. Shouldn't supervisors fear losing control of their staff members in an empowerment evaluation?

A. No. At first glance, it might appear that supervisors are superfluous because people are evaluating their own programs. However, as discussed earlier, empowerment evaluations are not conducted in a vacuum. People are still held accountable for the tasks they agreed to fulfill for a grant, an employer, or a volunteer service agency. Supervisors are still needed to be in control. However, in an empowerment evaluation, supervisors hold staff members accountable for what they said they would do to accomplish the same tasks required of their employment or service agreement. In many ways, it makes the supervisors' job easier or at least less stressful.

> Supervisors hold staff members accountable for what they said they would do.

Q. Do evaluators still have a job in an empowerment evaluation?

A. Yes. First, their job description shifts from the external expert to the internal critical friend, coach, and evaluation facilitator. Second, when community and staff members become capable of conducting their own evaluations, trained and experienced evaluators can operate at a much higher level of capacity and can actualize their own potential.

> In an empowerment evaluation, trained and experienced evaluators can actualize their own potential.

Q. Does empowerment evaluation diminish the role and authority of the evaluator?

A. On the contrary, empowerment evaluation empowers evaluators. Typically, people run when they see an evaluator coming their way. They generally have bad news about operation inefficiencies, deviations from the model, and inadequate performance; the list goes on with a sprinkling of positive comments and observations. In addition, community and staff members typically view evaluation as parasitic, reducing and diverting funds better served by staff members in directly related program operations and activities.

However, when community and staff members evaluate themselves, they turn to the empowerment evaluator (instead of running away) and ask how she can be helpful to them. The dynamic is positive and the evaluator's value (as a critical friend) is increased 10-fold.

> When community and staff members evaluate themselves, they turn to the empowerment evaluator (instead of running away) and ask how she can be helpful to them.

MULTIPLE PERSPECTIVES

Q. Have you ever had to deal with multiple perspectives in an empowerment evaluation, in which people have completely opposite viewpoints about the same issues?

A. Yes. This is precisely what empowerment evaluation is equipped to address and build on. Empowerment evaluations are as inclusive as possible. People are ideally ethnically and racially diverse and are recruited from all walks of life. The more comprehensive the stakeholder representation, the better. People are given the opportunity in an empowerment evaluation to see and hear different perspectives about the same program and the same problem. Solutions that surface from an exchange of contrasting perspectives have a higher probability of addressing systemic issues and meeting people's needs.

In addition, it is not uncommon for people to see patterns emerging from their Taking Stock exercise, highlighting contrasting perspectives. Administrators may have noticeably higher ratings than the rest of the group, in part because they operate at the more general policy level. Staff members operating at the ground level may be systematically more critical (and provide lower ratings) because they deal with implementation issues every day. Different perspectives and roles in an empowerment evaluation enrich the self-assessment, making solutions more credible and compelling.

> Solutions that surface from an exchange of contrasting perspectives have a higher probability of addressing systemic issues and meeting peoples' needs.

METHODOLOGICAL

Q. What is the difference between collaborative, participatory, and empowerment evaluation?

A. There are many similarities and differences between these stakeholder involvement approaches to evaluation. However, one way to highlight the difference between the approaches is to focus on the role of the evaluator. Collaborative evaluators are *in charge* of the evaluation, but they create an ongoing engagement between the evaluator and stakeholders. Participatory evaluators *jointly share* control of the evaluation. Empowerment evaluators view *program staff members, program participants, and community members as the ones in control of the evaluation.* However, empowerment evaluators serve as critical friends or coaches to help keep the process on track, rigorous, responsive, and relevant.

> Empowerment evaluators view program staff members, program participants, and community members as the ones in control of the evaluation.

Q. Do you agree with where Marvin Alkin (2013) put you on the evaluation tree?

A. Yes. Many colleagues argue that I belong on the methods part of the tree because of my contributions to methodology—for example, ethnography, qualitative methods, randomized controls, reactivity, online surveys, focus groups, informal interviews, and qualitative concepts ranging from contextualization and cultural interpretation to emic and etic perspectives of reality.

In fact, when I was much younger, my aunt Mary asked me at a Passover dinner what I did for a living, and I responded, "I am a methodologist." She sat puzzled and stared at me and responded, "Does that mean you are not Jewish anymore?" I reaffirmed my Jewish heritage and put her mind at ease. I also had to rethink my response. I realized, then and there, that I might have been preoccupied with methods, but my primary commitment was to use over methods, which is precisely where they put me. The fundamental question is: What do you do with the evaluative insights and findings once they are mined or derived from rigorous data collection and analysis? Use depends on quality methods, but in the end, at least for me, use is the point of most of our work.

> Use is the point of most of our work.

Q. Can empowerment evaluation be conducted with other forms of evaluation?

A. Yes. The W. K. Kellogg Foundation Board asked me to facilitate a multilevel and multidimensional empowerment evaluation throughout the foundation. However, in the middle of the empowerment evaluation, it was clear that one group only needed a collaborative evaluation. The two approaches complemented and enhanced each other.

> Empowerment and collaborative evaluation complement and enhance each other.

Q. Is empowerment evaluation a linear three-step process?

A. There are many ways to conduct an empowerment evaluation. There is a three-step (Mission, Taking Stock, Planning for the Future) and a 10-step (Getting to Outcomes) approach. In addition, some groups draw circles around their activities, such as communication, and place green dots (positive indicators) on the left side of the circles and red dots on the right side (highlighting prob-

> The aim is to complete the steps in order to help the group move from reflection to action.

lems). Each of these approaches has a linear logic in which the group moves from one step to the next. However, in reality each step requires detours and adaptations along the way. Nevertheless, the aim is to complete the steps in order to help the group move from reflection to action.

Q. Should the director or other powerful people be removed from the group's dialogue and discussions to get the most honest comments from the group?

A. No. I am often asked to remove a director or other leader. This results in a whining session. I need people to say what they are willing to say in front of the authorities they have to work with on a daily basis. Otherwise, they are just being set up for failure. If their supervisor is open to critique, high levels of empowerment evaluation can be conducted. If their supervisor is not open to debate and exchange, low levels of empowerment evaluation are more realistic. It should be noted that even low levels are better than none at all.

Q. Is empowerment evaluation methodologically agnostic?

A. Yes. It is qualitative in that people are asked to describe their Mission, to engage in dialogue about what's working and what might merit attention, and to Plan for the Future. However, prioritization, rating, and evaluation dashboards are typically quantitative. Moreover, the data required to monitor progress and evaluate performance are both qualitative and quantitative, depending on the specifics of the group's Plans for the Future.

> Both qualitative and quantitative data are required to monitor progress and evaluate performance.

PRACTICAL

Q. David, you can conduct an empowerment evaluation, but can I?

A. My colleagues and students often ask this question. My response is the same. You can conduct an empowerment evaluation. I can facilitate one better only because I have been conducting them for decades. A successful critical friend needs the temperament for it, including being respectful of others, being able to serve as a coach or critical friend (instead of directing the evaluation), and being open to diverse views and styles of communication.

Generally, however, I recommend that people work with someone more seasoned or offer their services with a "safe" group that they already know and trust. It is also prudent to secure a more seasoned empowerment evaluator and serve as an assistant if the group is a politically complex or powerful one.

Q. Can you conduct an empowerment evaluation in a hierarchical bureaucratic organization that is not philosophically aligned with empowerment evaluation principles?

A. Yes. Empowerment evaluations have been conducted with hierarchal bureaucratic organizations that are not philosophically aligned with empowerment evaluation principles. However, it takes longer, and the level of empowerment evaluation is much lower. My bias is to work with groups that are philosophically aligned with empowerment evaluation principles because you can get a lot more accomplished in less time. An argument could be made, however, that the hierarchical and bureaucratic organization needs assistance more than the more "progressive" ones—but that is a matter of personal choice, preference, and opportunity.

> You can get more accomplished in less time with groups that are philosophically aligned with empowerment evaluation principles.

Q. Why don't you just fire everyone and start over in low-performing communities and programs?

A. I often work in less than optimal conditions and places. They may be squatter settlements, rural and isolated communities, physically dangerous urban environments, and psychologically stressful contexts. Recruiting replacements is not a realistic option. In empowerment evaluation, with some exceptions, you work with the people you have. You help them harness their power to transform the circumstances and conditions they have inherited. You build capacity and foster self-determination.

> In empowerment evaluation, you work with the people you have.

Q. Do you punish people if they do not meet their milestones and goals?

A. No. The evaluation dashboard is designed to help people measure performance over time. If a group of people is not reaching its milestones or goals, people are not "slapped on the wrist," demonized, demoralized, or stigmatized. Their actual performance is compared with their milestones and goals. Failure to meet milestones is simply a "flag" that they need help.

> The evaluation dashboard is designed to help people measure performance over time.

They use it to monitor themselves. In addition, the evaluator, administrative group, and donor have access to that information. There is typically someone in the community who has been successful at the task, and can be asked to share what she is doing and possibly to work with the "underachieving" or less-successful group. Alternatively, external experts might be solicited to assist the group. The evaluation measurements are used to learn from the experience and make midcourse corrections in order to accomplish desired goals, results, and/or outcomes.

Q. Can I use empowerment evaluation with my family?

A. Yes. Although it is primarily used with community groups and organizations, families can use empowerment evaluation to address domestic concerns in their homes, faith-based institutions, and social clubs. I used it at a family reunion. Our kids and nieces and nephews were given the opportunity to select a summer activity together. Most of my younger relatives chose conventional summertime activities, including swimming, baseball, going to the movies, getting ice cream, and making candles.

My daughter saw a truck filled with cucumbers and said she wanted us to go pick cucumbers in the hot, humid summer fields of New England. Empowerment evaluation turned out to be invaluable. The kids made a list of the activities they wanted to pursue. I gave all the kids some dots. They decided where we should go and what we should do. As hard as it is to believe, almost no one selected picking cucumbers during a hot New England summer. I looked great because I did not have to be the dad who decided that his daughter's selection was less than optimal. She learned that she had to work with the will of her cousins.

Q. Does empowerment evaluation only work in one kind of organization?

A. No. The same approach has been used in a wide variety of programs and settings. We work in over 17 countries, as mentioned earlier. Organizations range from high-tech companies in Silicon Valley to townships in South Africa. Our programs include tobacco prevention, addiction studies, food justice, TB elimination, sex education, science education, and substance abuse. The settings include Native American reservations, medical schools, graduate schools, elementary and secondary schools, hospitals, architectural firms, and senior centers. The approach is essentially the same, with minor adaptations. The commitment to capacity building and outcomes is the same in all applications, programs, initiatives, and settings.

Q. How do you work with institutional ethics committees, such as the institutional review board (IRB), when you don't know what questions you will be asking in advance?

A. We work closely with IRBs. The approach is similar to that of qualitative study reviews, in which you submit probable grand-tour questions at each stage of your inquiry with probable follow-up questions (Fetterman, 2020). Empowerment evaluation is somewhat easier to present to the IRB because it has specific activities you can describe in advance (without knowing what the group's response will be in advance), including (1) Mission, (2) Taking Stock, and (3) Planning for the Future. In addition, many of the critical questions are known in advance, such as:

"What is your Mission?"

"What are the most important activities your organization is engaged in to reach the Mission?"

"How well does your organization conduct the most important activities?"

"What do you plan to do to improve your program in the future?"

"What are your group's goals and strategies for accomplishing your Plans for the Future, and what is the evidence used to determine if the group is implementing its strategies and that they are effective?"

"Are you reaching your milestones and goals?"

"What are you going to do to reach your milestones and goals?"

The list of questions continues, but empowerment evaluation provides IRBs with sufficient information for a complete or expedited review.

Q. Can you invite an external agency to contribute a "second set of eyes" in an empowerment evaluation?

A. Yes. We often have external teams visit and provide a "second set of eyes" on our work. The key is to invite them to review your work on your terms and according to the appropriate organizational stage of development. Too many external reviewers have the best of intentions and destroy a program because their assessment is off target. They may evaluate the group or agency as if it is an organizationally fully functioning and mature operation, working at full capacity, when in fact the program is in its organizational infancy and just barely getting off the ground. In addition to being unfair and inaccurate, this external team can divert needed funds from pressing concerns that should be addressed at the moment.

> We often have external teams visit and provide a "second set of eyes" on our work.

Q. Can you provide us with examples of the cultural norms you work with?

A. Native American tribes typically require permission from the elders to conduct an empowerment evaluation on a reservation. The elders are also called on to make the blessings and benedictions at meals, and they review and approve of all documents shared with the public. In Black communities, pastors need to be consulted and recruited to help in social welfare programs.

Gangs need to be consulted to obtain permission for prospective students to attend programs for dropouts in their neighborhoods. In some cases, permission depends on following a gang's rules to the letter—for example, prohibiting students from wearing certain colored clothing so they can safely navigate through a gang's neighborhood territories.

Empowerment evaluators need permission from school superintendents to facilitate empowerment evaluations in their school districts.

In Iran, empowerment evaluators respect the cultural and religious norms that prohibit men and women from physically interacting with each other. They have the men sit on one side of the room and the women on the other side. The men are called up to place their "dots" on the poster paper to prioritize the list of activities they will rate and discuss. Next, the women are invited to participate in the same manner. In this way, their "minds" or thoughts are shared on the same piece of paper (with the dots combined), while the prohibitions and restrictions of the group or culture are respected.

MECHANICAL

Q. Does everyone have to be present at the same time and in the same place?

A. No. We work in hospitals, and it is impossible for all the nurses and physicians to be physically present at the same time. In hospital settings, even pre-COVID, we operated online. Everyone was given the opportunity to prioritize, rate, and discuss in an asynchronous fashion.

Similarly, in educational institutions, it is almost impossible to bring everyone together simultaneously in the same place. We brought sheets of poster paper with partially completed ratings to secretaries, janitors, and other workers who were unable to attend the primary sessions together. Our empowerment evaluation of the Mars rover program was conducted completely online since we were unable to gather all the students together from across the country in the same place simultaneously. I have also conducted empowerment evaluations with over 50 computer science educational evaluators. We have never met as a group in real time and in the same location. We did not have the funds or the time to conduct the self-assessment together. However, most of them conducted all of the work online, so an empowerment evaluation conducted remotely felt normal.

Q. Is it okay to use a zero rating?

A. No. Everyone has an opinion, an impression, and a rationale for their rating. It is important to share that impression with the group, even if it is off target, because sharing it highlights how the program or activity is perceived. I remember that one of the secretaries at a school I was teaching at said she could not rate the teachers because she never observed any of us teaching. I said that I remembered standing in the hallway next to her office, listening to her counsel a student on the best courses to take based on what she knew about faculty members' reputations. Her impression of teaching at the institution shaped student opinion and choice and thus was as important as direct observation of teaching.

> It is important to share impressions because sharing them highlights how the program or activity is perceived.

Q. Do you exclude the extremists in the community?

A. No. I invite stakeholders who are extremist. They can open up conversations. The group might think that speaking about staffing imbalances is too sensitive to discuss in an open-group setting. However, when a blustery, somewhat insensitive, member of the group (prone to exaggeration) makes allegations of corruption and mismanagement, a discussion of staffing becomes fair game and is a much less threatening or sensitive topic. These stakeholders raise the ceiling in terms of what's safe or acceptable to speak about. In addition, they are often prone to exaggeration and hyperbole because they have been marginalized and disregarded for many years as a result of sexism, racism, and/or ageism. Invited, they may become zealots and converts and major supporters of the empowerment evaluation initiative. Uninvited, they may undermine the engagement.

Q. When is the best time to begin an empowerment evaluation?

A. Like most evaluations, it is best to begin at the beginning, when the program or initiative is first conceived and implemented. However, one of the benefits of empowerment evaluation is that it can be used at any stage of development or implementation.

It can be used to help plan and develop a program. It can be used in the middle of an evaluation to create a baseline, a Plan for the Future, and milestones and goals. Ironically, it can be used when a traditional evaluation cannot be used at all—at the end of a program. When a program ends, through empowerment evaluation a group can determine what it needs to do next to remain sustainable, including a frantic search for continued funding. It can also be used at this time to make plans to decommission the initiative and collect the lessons learned retrospectively.

People have asked if was best to wait until COVID was over or until the dust settled concerning political controversies and/or economic disasters. The answer was and continues to be no. Temporal conditions should never be used to delay an empowerment evaluation. There will always be a problem, a catastrophe, or a destabilizing activity. There is never a perfect time to begin an empowerment evaluation.

Our efforts to eliminate TB in India continued throughout the worst periods of COVID in India and the United States. In fact, we expanded our reach because Zoom and other videoconference software had become the norm for communication and facilitation. We were able to attract an even larger population than we would have if we were limited to face-to-face interactions. In this case, the tragedy of COVID, although painful, allowed us to expand our reach exponentially.

Q. Why are you so open to critique?

A. First, we are open to critique because we might be wrong, and second, because we may learn something to improve and refine our efforts. Edmund Burke said, "He [or she] that wrestles with us strengthens our nerves and sharpens our skills. Our antagonist is our helper."

7

Conclusion

Commitments to Social Justice

Justice does not mean "just us"; it is meant for all of us.

Evaluation and social justice can, has, and should continue to go hand in hand. The time is always right to take a position against the culture of silence that allows injustice and inequities to persist. Empowerment evaluation has been used as one sword, among many, in the fight for social justice. Examples highlighted in this chapter include helping keep minority youth away from tobacco (Fetterman, 2015b), providing comprehensive sex education to reduce unintended teen pregnancy and HIV/STI rates (Dugan, 2018), raising test scores and increasing student learning in impoverished and formerly segregated rural schools in academic distress (Fetterman, 2005b), and bridging the digital divide in communities of color (Fetterman, 2013a). Food insecurity/food justice and TB elimination, the case examples also highlighted in this discussion, represent additional powerful examples of empowerment evaluation's commitment to social justice principles in practice.

> The time is always right to take a position against the culture of silence that allows injustice and inequities to persist.

A brief review of these examples is presented to highlight empowerment evaluation's long-term commitment to social justice. It is followed by a few observations concerning empowerment evaluation's evolution. Finally, the book comes full circle, as I take empowerment evaluation back to its roots and bring additional conceptual clarity and closure.

TOBACCO PREVENTION AND CESSATION

Tobacco is the leading cause of preventable death in the world, according to the WHO (2008). The CDC (2011) found that "tobacco use is the single most preventable cause of disease, disability, and death in the United States" (p. 1). It is responsible for more deaths than AIDS, alcohol, car accidents, illegal drugs, murders, and suicides combined (Campaign for Tobacco-Free Kids, 2014).

Tobacco use is a major contributor to death among African Americans, specifically in the areas of heart disease, cancer, and stroke. According to the CDC (2019), African Americans are more likely to die from smoking-related diseases than Whites, even though they smoke fewer cigarettes and start smoking at an older age. In addition, there is a 30–40% increased risk of developing diabetes for cigarette smokers as compared with nonsmokers (CDC, 2018). This statistic is significant because diabetes is the fourth leading cause of death among African Americans (U.S. Department of Health and Human Services, 2014). (See also American Lung Association, 2010; Kochanek, Murphy, Xu, & Tejada-Vera, 2016; Schoenborn, Adams, & Peregoy, 2013; U.S. Department of Health and Human Services, 1998.)

> "Tobacco use is the single most preventable cause of disease, disability, and death in the United States" (CDC, 2011, p. 1). It is responsible for more deaths than AIDS, alcohol, car accidents, illegal drugs, murders, and suicides combined.

These statistics are compounded by an equally aggressive tobacco industry marketing campaign directed at African Americans. The industry disproportionately advertises in African American publications, exposing Blacks to more tobacco-related advertisements than Whites (U.S. Department of Health and Human Services, 1998). It is no accident that 9 out of 10 African American smokers prefer menthol cigarettes (Giovino, et al., 2015; Villanti, et al., 2017). Menthol tobacco should no longer be used as a weapon to kill BIPOC populations.

> More than eight out of 10 Black smokers use menthol cigarettes, in part because of targeted advertisements and promotions from tobacco companies. As a result, these individuals incur more of the health consequences from smoking than other races and ethnicities. A 2021 study found that although Black Americans make up 12 percent of the population, they incurred 41 percent of all deaths and 50 percent of the years of life lost due to menthol cigarettes between 1980 and 2018. (Foley & Daniels, 2022)

The Arkansas Department of Health allocated a portion of the Master Tobacco Settlement Agreement (1998) to the Minority Initiative Sub-Recipient Grant Office (MISRGO) at the University of Arkansas at Pine Bluff to combat these grim statistics. MISGRO in turn awarded grants to more than 100 Arkansas organizations for tobacco prevention and cessation programs. The grantees ranged from faith-based agencies to hospitals. Most of them have been community-based social service agencies.

> "More than eight out of 10 Black smokers use menthol cigarettes, in part because of targeted advertisements and promotions from tobacco companies. As a result, these individuals incur more of the health consequences from smoking than other races and ethnicities" (Foley & Daniels, 2022).

Empowerment Evaluation

MISRGO and its grantees have applied a three-step empowerment evaluation approach for over a decade (Fetterman, 2015b). These community-based organizations have used empowerment evaluation to help produce a steady stream of accomplishments. They include policy changes on the state level, such as the passage of Act 811 in 2011, which imposed sanctions for smoking in a vehicle with a child under the age of 14. It has also been useful in helping communities strengthen Arkansas's smoke-free car law (Act 13 of 2006), increasing the age of children protected from secondhand smoke from age 6 to 14, impacting more than 827,411 children. Empowerment evaluation dashboards have also helped grantees successfully create smoke-free parks across the state and increase the number of people pledging to quit smoking. MISRGO, MISRGO grantees, and the empowerment evaluation team translated the number of youth they stopped from smoking into dollars, saving the state more than $84 million in excess medical expenses.

MISRGO grantees have also turned to empowerment evaluation dashboards to monitor their use of newspaper, radio, and television media to successfully communicate with the public. Through their media campaigns (and quarterly monitoring of their evaluation dashboards), they have substantially contributed to smokers calling the Quitline to assist them in their efforts to stop smoking. These efforts are all in alignment with the CDC guidelines and recommendations: "State tobacco quitlines provide evidence-based, cost-effective cessation services to hundreds of thousands of people each year over the phone, web, and other communication channels" (CDC, 2020, p. 27).

External evaluations of the tobacco-prevention work in Arkansas also suggest that the grantees have been effective. For example, cigarette use has been cut by one-third in the state according to a 10-year study conducted by the RAND Corporation (Engberg, Scharf, Lovejoy, Yu, & Tharp-Taylor, 2012). Reductions have been particularly significant in the Delta, a region of the state with a high minority population.

COMPREHENSIVE SEX EDUCATION

Approximately half of all pregnancies across the globe, or 121 million pregnancies, are unintended, according to the United Nation's Population Fund (UNFPA). Unintended pregnancies are more likely to happen in poor communities where women lack sufficient education (or access to services). "This is a crisis that's all around us," according to UNFPA Executive Director Natalia Kanem (Roth, 2022, p. 1). "But it's unseen. It's unrecognized and that is part of a global failure to prioritize women and girls and to uphold the basic human rights for women and adolescents" (p. 1).

> Approximately half of all pregnancies across the globe, or 121 million pregnancies, are unintended. Unintended pregnancies are more likely to happen in poor communities where women lack sufficient education (or access to services).

Multiple methods for contraception exist to minimize unwanted pregnancies. However, many women are prevented from using contraception. In some cases, women using contraception are stigmatized. Contraception can also fail: 13% of women using condoms will become pregnant. This problem is compounded by misconceptions about contraception and sex education, including the belief that perimenopausal women think they don't need it. Sex education is one of the most promising paths forward to confront ignorance and respond to this basic human rights issue. A state-funded sex education initiative was implemented in Colorado to partly address this crisis.

Empowerment Evaluation

This sex education team was responsible for its own program evaluation. The team selected empowerment evaluation and learned by doing and receiving information along the way. The empowerment evaluation included analyzing meeting minutes and conducting archival studies, learning circles, focus groups, online surveys, and one-to-one interviews.

The evaluation also relied on infographics to tell the community's stories.

The results of the empowerment evaluation's pre–post survey were positive. Eighty-four percent of the youth intend to use birth control, and 17% said they were less likely to engage in sex for the remainder of the year (6 months). The empowerment evaluation made significant contributions to the impact of the initiative on many levels as well, including:

1. Implementing sex education programs in schools where administrators and school boards were reluctant to do so
2. Building the social infrastructure required to conduct comprehensive sex education classes
3. Developing more effective state- and countywide unintended teen-pregnancy prevention efforts
4. Cultivating community support for the program

ACADEMIC DISTRESS

The Arkansas Delta is one of the most impoverished and isolated areas in the country. In addition, the southern Delta communities were segregated by law in the past. Blacks went to one school, while Whites went to another. The discrepancy between the education provided Blacks and Whites in terms of facilities, textbooks, and teachers was stark and incontestable. The legacy of this separate-and-unequal educational opportunity in the past continues to the present, most visibly in terms of student test scores.

The Arkansas Delta school districts were classified as being in "academic distress," which means that more than 40% of the students in the district are at or below the 25th percentile on the statewide assessment. The state had the right to "take over" the districts. However, firing the administrators and teachers was not desirable or even possible. The remote and isolated nature of the impoverished communities made it difficult to recruit credentialed teachers, thus making building capacity with the existing teachers and administrators a necessary. Therefore, we stepped up and negotiated a "partnership."

> The discrepancy between the education provided Blacks and Whites in terms of facilities, textbooks, and teachers is stark and incontestable. The legacy of this separate-and-unequal educational opportunity in the past continues to the present, most visibly in terms of student test scores.

Empowerment Evaluation

The Arkansas empowerment evaluation represented a clear commitment to social justice, focusing on people who were long deprived of access to basic educational opportunities. The primary outcome was to raise student test scores and increase learning. According to Arkansas Department of Education educational accountability officials who partnered in the effort, "Empowerment evaluation was instrumental in producing Elaine and Altheimer school district improvement, including raising student test scores" (Smith, 2004; Wilson, 2004). At the beginning of the intervention, 50% of the Elaine School District students scored below the 25th percentile on the Stanford 9 Achievement Test. By the end of the empowerment evaluation intervention, only 38.5% of students scored below the 25th percentile, representing an improvement of more than 20 percentage points. Similar gains were made in the Altheimer Unified School District.

The media, both television and print, reported on the positive gains as well. Parents, teachers, students, and administrators held themselves accountable for improving discipline, parental involvement, community participation, and governance and management. Gains were made in each of the activities selected by the districts.

BRIDGING THE DIGITAL DIVIDE

HP's $15-million Digital Village project was designed to help three minority communities, largely left behind in the digital age, leapfrog across the digital divide. Two communities were located on the West Coast, and one was located on the East Coast.

The Tribal Digital Village was one of the Hewlett-Packard Digital Village communities. It consisted of 18 American Indian tribes in California. The project addressed a variety of social justice issues. Equity in education, housing, employment, and health care were paramount. The preservation of the tribes' rich cultural heritage was another goal that was interwoven throughout the fabric of their project.

> HP's $15-million Digital Village project was designed to help three minority communities, largely left behind in the digital age, leapfrog across the digital divide.

The focus on the tribes' heritage took on particular significance because of American Indians' previous treatment by the Bureau of Indian

Affairs (BIA). The BIA took children away from their homes and enrolled them in boarding schools where they were separated from their communities and culture. In addition, they were routinely prohibited from speaking their native language. The phys-ical layout of the reservation itself functioned to isolate individuals, inhibit communication, and fragment cultural knowledge. The Tribal Digital Village participants contributed to the preservation and maintenance of Native cultures. They also took another step into the digital age.

> The BIA took children away from their homes and enrolled them in boarding schools where they were separated from their communities and culture. In addition, they were routinely prohibited from speaking their native language.

Empowerment Evaluation

The Tribal Digital Village used empowerment evaluation to help create the largest unlicensed wireless system in the country at the time. Participants used empowerment evaluation dashboards to start a high-resolution printing press business. In addition, they addressed equity issues by providing young people with computer training that enabled them to maintain the wireless system they constructed. This training represented an investment in their future as well as in their past. It helped make social justice initiatives sustainable from one generation to the next.

HP understood the philosophy behind empowerment evaluation and demonstrated respect for community ownership from the inception of the project, allowing the Tribal Digital Village members to design and conduct their evaluations with the assistance of the empowerment evaluation team. The Digital Village was in charge of the content of every stage of the evaluation. Participants produced, with the assistance of their empowerment evaluators, online surveys, training programs for collecting stories from their elders, digital photographs showing them constructing their wireless transmission towers, and QuickTime videos of the critical stages of the evaluation.

The Tribal Digital Village also reflexively demonstrated its accomplishments by teaching one of my empowerment evaluation classes. Participants videoconferenced with my Stanford University students from the community's towers. The community's members had internalized the practical aspects of evaluation well enough to teach about it. Moreover, they were teaching about it using the very tools they had made a commitment to build. The Digital Village held itself accountable and produced concrete outcomes.

TB ELIMINATION

TB is the leading lethal infectious disease in the world. In 2018, 23% of the world's population was infected by TB bacteria (CDC, 2022). Eight countries account for two-thirds of the total cases, including India, China, Indonesia, the Philippines, Pakistan, Nigeria, Bangladesh, and South Africa. India has the world's largest TB epidemic (26% of TB cases across the globe), according to the WHO (2021).

The United States, in contrast, has one of the lowest TB rates. However, 89% of the TB cases in the United States occurred among racial and ethnic minority groups in 2020; 71.5% of cases were non-U.S.-born persons in 2020 (CDC, 2022).

> TB is the leading lethal infectious disease in the world. India has the world's largest TB epidemic.

Empowerment Evaluation

Chapter 4 presented a case example that highlighted empowerment evaluation contributions to eliminating TB in India. The USAID-funded REACH effort is attuned to national policy and values local community-led responses to TB. One of the empowerment evaluation focal points is preparing TB Champions to advocate for TB rights in the health care system.

FOOD INSECURITY/FOOD JUSTICE

Food insecurity is also a social justice issue. There are over 38 million people experiencing food insecurity in the United States. This figure includes over 12 million children. The suffering is not evenly distributed. According to Feeding America (2022), "In 2021, 20% of Black individuals experienced *food insecurity*—more than three times the rate of White households."

> There are over 38 million people experiencing food insecurity in the United States. This figure includes over 12 million children.

Empowerment Evaluation

Chapter 3 presented another case example of the link between evaluation and social justice, that of food insecurity and food justice in the United States. As discussed earlier, Feeding America is partnering with Starbucks to help 15 food banks apply a racial equity lens to their work. Empowerment evaluation is one of the tools used to help grantees apply this lens, with the aim of reducing food insecurity and promoting food justice. The work is being completed remotely, creating grantee empowerment evaluation dashboards online using Google Sheets.

EQUITY AND JUSTICE

Equity and justice are not static concepts or values. They are evolving. We are working with our best understanding of what equity and justice mean and to whom these concepts apply. This shapes our efforts to measure, monitor, and evaluate change over time (Romans, Stancieland, & Harley, 2022). The answers to these definitional questions will continue to be imperfect and insufficient. Historically, however, equity and justice were rarely a part of the conversation. The culture of silence had implications for program implementation and evaluation, particularly for BIPOC populations.

> Equity and justice are evolving concepts.

The conversation has evolved. New terms and concepts have emerged and inform our discourse. For example, *decolonizing* data or returning collected data to BIPOC communities—the rightful owners—help them make informed decisions and guide research practice in the process (Ramanathan, Fruchterman, Fowler, & Carotti-Sha, 2022). *Positionality* as a methodology was also largely absent from our methodological discourse in the past. According to Duarte (2017, p. 135), positionality "requires researchers to identify their own degrees of privilege through factors of race, class, educational attainment, income, ability, gender, and citizenship, among others." Its purpose is to help researchers reflect on and understand how their positions in society influence their work, understandings, and actions in an inequitable world.

Intersectionality "describes the ways in which systems of inequality based on gender, race, ethnicity, sexual orientation, gender identity, disability, class and other forms of discrimination 'intersect' to create unique dynamics and effects" (Center for Intersectional Justice, 2022). Intersectionality expands our understanding of injustice. It draws attention to the compounding and reinforcing nature of discrimination in society (Collins, 2001).

Empowerment evaluation has been used as a sword in the fight for social justice. It has helped to bring many of these conversations among previously marginalized and devalued groups as well as researchers and evaluators to the table. Moreover, empowerment evaluation places BIPOC populations in the driver's seat, empowering them to define equity and justice and to measure it themselves.

COMING FULL CIRCLE

It is only fitting that this discussion conclude precisely where it began almost 30 years ago. Empowerment evaluation was birthed in excitement, anticipation, exhilaration, and trepidation. The atmosphere at my 1993 AEA presidential address was electric. Empowerment evaluation was rapidly embraced by communities across the globe. It resonated with their own practices. It legitimated what many people were already doing—self-evaluation—but in a more systematic and grounded manner.

> Empowerment evaluation was birthed in excitement, anticipation, exhilaration, and trepidation. It was viewed as a threat to the status quo. It is now part of the intellectual landscape of evaluation.

However, it also faced harsh resistance and even personal attacks. It was viewed as a threat to the status quo. My response to these accusations was to agree with our critics' deepest fears. In my presidential address I said, "Colleagues who fear that we are giving evaluation away are right. We are sharing it with a broader population. Those who fear that we are educating ourselves out of a job are only partially correct" (Fetterman, 1994). Wild's observation (1997, p. 172), as noted in Chapter 1, captured the tone of the time: "Fetterman et al. have nailed their theses to the door of the cathedral. Now the question is, how tolerant is the establishment of dissent?"

Fast forward a couple of decades later, to when empowerment evaluation celebrated its 21st anniversary at the 2015 AEA meeting (Fetterman & Wandersman, 2017). Luminaries in the field who helped shape empowerment evaluation with their critiques, concerns, and appreciation celebrated empowerment evaluation's contributions.

I thank each and every one of my colleagues for their contributions over the last almost 3 decades. They have helped empowerment evaluation build capacity, foster self-determination, and contribute to social justice. I look forward to continuing the dialogue and development. Patton's closing remarks at our empowerment evaluation anniversary session continues to be appropriate: "Today we are celebrating 21 impressive years of making contributions to evaluation practice and theory . . . let's shoot for the big 50th anniversary" (Patton, 2017, p. 140). I look forward to continuing the dialogue as we reflect on and refine empowerment evaluation's evolution and contribution to theory and practice.

Glossary of Terms

Conscientização or **conscientization**—the process by which communities develop a critical understanding of their social reality through reflection and action.

Culture of silence—acquiescence to a pervasive system of beliefs and ideologies that undermine and devalue entire groups of people.

Decolonizing data—returning collected data to BIPOC communities to help them make informed decisions.

Empowerment evaluation—the use of evaluation concepts, techniques, and findings to foster improvement and self-determination. It is an approach that aims to increase the likelihood that programs will achieve results by increasing the capacity of program stakeholders to plan, implement, and evaluate their own programs

> **Practical empowerment evaluation**—an approach designed to enhance program performance and productivity. It is controlled by program staff, participants, and community members. However, the focus is on practical problem solving, as well as on programmatic improvements and outcomes.

> **Transformative empowerment evaluation**—an approach that highlights the psychological, social, and political power of liberation. People learn how to take greater control of their own lives and the resources around them. The focus in transformative empowerment evaluation is on liberation from predetermined, conventional roles and organizational structures or "ways of doing things." In addition, empowerment is a more explicit and apparent goal.

Flexnerian model—a traditional medical education model, with 2 years of science and then 2 years of clinical work.

Food insecurity—the lack of consistent access to enough food for every person in a household to live an active and healthy life.

Food justice—healthy food is viewed as a human right. The movement was founded to combat structural racism and promote access to resources, focusing on the distribution of food within low-income communities. The larger politics of food production are not always challenged.

Food security—both physical and economic access to sufficient food to meet dietary needs for a productive and healthy life.

Food sovereignty—healthy and culturally appropriate food is viewed as a human right. In addition, people have the right to determine their own food and agricultural production systems. The movement was founded by peasant farmers and calls for equal and democratized food production systems. In addition, food should be produced using ecologically sound and sustainable methods.

Freirean pedagogy—a teaching philosophy that invites educators to encourage students to question the status quo, critique existing power structures, and assert their rights. It is a philosophy of liberation in which people are responsible for taking charge of their own lives and leading the effort to liberate themselves. It is the opposite of traditional pedagogies, often referred to as the "banking model of education," which view students as empty vessels to be filled with facts and knowledge. Freirean pedagogy views the learner as a co-creator of knowledge.

Guided immersion—a learning approach in which people conduct their own evaluation (immersed in the experience), assisted (or guided) by an empowerment evaluator.

Intersectionality—a concept that describes the ways in which systems of inequality based on gender, race, ethnicity, sexual orientation, gender identity, disability, class and other forms of discrimination "intersect" to create complex and compounded forms of inequities and injustices.

Positionality—the context that defines one's identity and requires researchers to identify and state their own degrees of privilege, typically based on race, class, educational attainment, income, ability, gender, and citizenship.

Social justice—the principle of respecting and protecting everyone's human rights. It is fundamentally about fairness. A few of the most pressing social justice issues include racial equity, gender equality, and LGBTQ+ rights.

References

Alkin, M., & Christie, C. (2004). An evaluation theory tree. In M. Alkin (Ed.), *Evaluation roots: Tracing theorists' views and influences*. Thousand Oaks, CA: SAGE.

American Lung Association. (2010). *Too many cases, too many deaths: Lung cancer in African Americans*. Washington, DC: Author. Retrieved June 12, 2018, from *http://tobaccopolicycenter.org/wp-content/uploads/2017/11/041.pdf*.

Argyris, C., & Schon, D. A. (1978). *Organizational learning: A theory of action perspective*. Reading, MA: Addison-Wesley.

Burke, E. (1790). *Reflections on the revolution in France, and on the proceedings in certain societies in London relative to that event: In a letter intended to have been sent to a gentleman in Paris*. Ireland: J. Dodsley.

Campaign for Tobacco-Free Kids. (2014). The toll of tobacco in Arkansas. Retrieved from *www.tobaccofreekids.org/facts_issues/toll_us/arkansas*.

Center for Intersectional Justice. (2022). What is intersectionality? Retrieved from *www.intersectionaljustice.org/what-is-intersectionality*.

Centers for Disease Control and Prevention. (2018). African Americans and tobacco use. Retrieved from *www.cdc.gov/tobacco/disparities/african-americans/index.htm*.

Centers for Disease Control and Prevention. (2019). Tuberculosis health disparities. Retrieved from *www.cdc.gov/tb/topic/populations/healthdisparities/default.htm*.

Centers for Disease Control and Prevention. (2020). *Best practices user guide: Cessation in tobacco prevention control*. Atlanta: U.S. Department of Health and Human Services, Centers for Disease Control and Prevention, National Center for Chronic Disease Prevention and Health Promotion, Office on Smoking and Health.

Centers for Disease Control and Prevention, Global Health. (2019). Tuberculosis. Retrieved from *www.cdc.gov/globalhealth/newsroom/topics/ tb/index.html#:~:text=What%20is%20the%20global%20impact,1.5%20 million%20lives%20each%20year.*

Centers for Disease Control and Prevention, Health Disparities. (2022). Tuberculosis. Retrieved from at *www.cdc.gov/tb/topic/populations/ healthdisparities/default.htm#:~:text=Racial%20and%20Ethnic%20 Disparities,-TB%20adversely%20affects&text=In%202020%2C%20 about%2089%25%20of,national%20case%20total%20in%202020.*

Centers for Disease Control and Prevention, National Center for Chronic Disease Prevention and Health Promotion. (2011). *Tobacco use: Targeting the nation's leading killer.* Atlanta, GA: Author.

Christie, C. A., & Alkin, M. (Ed.). (2013). An evaluation theory tree. In M. Alkin, (Ed)., *Evaluation roots: A wider perspective of theorists' views and influences* (2nd ed.). Thousand Oaks, CA: SAGE.

Clinton, J., & Hattie, J. (2015). Teachers as evaluators: An empowerment evaluation approach. In D. M. Fetterman, S. Kaftarian, & A. Wandersman (Eds.), *Empowerment evaluation: Knowledge and tools for self-assessment, evaluation capacity building, and accountability* (2nd ed.). Thousand Oaks, CA: SAGE.

Coleman-Jensen, A., Rabbitt, M. P., Gregory, C. A., & Singh, A. (2021). *Household food security in the United States in 2020, ERR-298.* Washington, DC: U.S. Department of Agriculture, Economic Research Service.

Collins, P. H. (2001). *Black feminist thought: Knowledge, consciousness, and the politics of empowerment.* New York: Routledge.

Datta, L. (2016). [Review of the book *Empowerment evaluation: Knowledge and tools for self-assessment, evaluation capacity building, and accountability* (2nd ed.) by D. M. Fetterman, S. Kaftarian, & A. Wandersman (Eds.)]. *American Journal of Evaluation, 38*(2), 294–299.

Datta, L. (2018). [Amazon review of the book *Collaborative, participatory, and empowerment evaluation: Stakeholder involvement approaches* by D. M. Fetterman, L. Rodríguez-Campos, A. P. Zukoski, & Contributors (Eds.)]. New York: Guilford Press.

Delwiche L. D., & Slaughter, S. J. (2019). *The little SAS® book: A primer* (6th ed.). Cary, NC: SAS Institute.

Donaldson, S. (2015). Foreword. In D. M. Fetterman, S. Kaftarian, & A. Wandersman (Eds.), *Empowerment evaluation: Knowledge and tools for self-assessment, evaluation capacity building, and accountability* (2nd ed.). Thousand Oaks, CA: SAGE.

Donaldson, S. I. (2017). Empowerment evaluation: An approach that has literally altered the landscape of evaluation. *Evaluation and Program Planning, 63,* 136–137.

Donaldson, S. I., Patton, M. Q., Fetterman, D., & Scriven, M. (2010). The 2009

Claremont debates: The promise and pitfalls of utilization-focused and empowerment evaluation. *Journal of MultiDisciplinary Evaluation, 6*(13), 15–57. (See debate at *http://cgu.edu/pages/6494.asp*.)

Duarte, M. E. (2017). *Network sovereignty: Building the internet across Indian country.* Seattle: University of Washington Press.

Duffy, J. L., & Wandersman, A. (2007, November). *A review of research on evaluation capacity building strategies.* Paper presented at the annual conference of the American Evaluation Association, Baltimore, MD.

Dugan, M. (2018). An empowerment evaluation of a comprehensive sex education initiative. In D. M. Fetterman, L. Rodríguez-Campos, A. P. Zukoski, & Contributors (Eds.), *Collaborative, participatory, and empowerment evaluation: Stakeholder involvement approaches* (pp. 90–104). New York: Guilford Press.

Engberg, J., Scharf, D. M., Lovejoy, S. L., Yu, H., & Tharp-Taylor, S. (2012). *Evaluation of the Arkansas Tobacco Settlement Program: Progress through 2011.* Santa Monica, CA: RAND Corporation.

Evergreen, S. D. (2017). *Effective data visualization: The right chart for the right data.* Thousand Oaks, CA: SAGE.

Evergreen, S. D. (2018). *Presenting data effectively: Communicating your findings for maximum impact.* Thousand Oaks, CA: SAGE.

Feeding America. (2022). Black communities face many unique challenges that result in being more likely to face hunger during the pandemic. Retrieved from *www.feedingamerica.org/hunger-in-america/african-american*.

Fetterman, D. M. (1981). Blaming the victim: The problem of evaluation design and federal involvement, and reinforcing world views in education. *Human Organization, 40,* 67–77.

Fetterman, D. M. (1989). *Ethnography: Step by step.* Thousand Oaks, CA: SAGE.

Fetterman, D. M. (1994). Empowerment evaluation: 1993 Presidential address. *Evaluation Practice, 15*(1), 1–15.

Fetterman, D. M. (1995). In response to Dr. Daniel Stufflebeam's: Empowerment evaluation, objectivist evaluation, and evaluation standards: Where the future of evaluation should not go and where it needs to go, October 1994, 321–338. *Evaluation Practice, 16*(2), 179–199.

Fetterman, D. M. (1998). *Ethnography: Step by step* (2nd ed.). Thousand Oaks, CA: SAGE.

Fetterman, D. M. (2001a). *Foundations of empowerment evaluation.* Thousand Oaks, CA: SAGE.

Fetterman, D. M. (2001b). The World Wide Web: Using the internet as a tool to disseminate empowerment evaluation worldwide. In D. M. Fetterman *Foundations of empowerment evaluation.* Thousand Oaks, CA: SAGE.

Fetterman, D. M. (2004a). Empowerment evaluation. In S. Mathison (Ed.), *Encyclopedia of evaluation.* Thousand Oaks, CA: SAGE.

Fetterman, D. M. (2004b). Empowerment evaluation. In A. R. Roberts & K. R.

Yeager (Eds.), *Evidence-based practice manual: Research outcome measures in health and human services*. Oxford, UK: Oxford University Press.

Fetterman, D. M. (2005a). A window into the heart and soul of empowerment evaluation. In D. M. Fetterman & A. Wandersman (Eds.), *Empowerment evaluation principles in practice*. New York: Guilford Press.

Fetterman, D. M. (2005b). Empowerment evaluation: From the digital divide to academic distress. In D. M. Fetterman & A. Wandersman (Eds.), *Empowerment evaluation principles in practice*. New York: Guilford Press.

Fetterman, D. M. (2009a). Empowerment evaluation at the Stanford University School of Medicine: Using a critical friend to improve the clerkship experience. *Ensaio, 17*(63), 197–204.

Fetterman, D. M. (2009b). *Ethnography: Step by step* (3rd ed.). Thousand Oaks, CA: SAGE.

Fetterman, D. M. (2012). Empowerment evaluation and accreditation case examples: California Institute of Integral Studies and Stanford University. In C. Secolsky (Ed.), *Measurement and evaluation in higher education*. London: Routledge.

Fetterman, D. M. (2013a). *Empowerment evaluation in the Digital Villages: Hewlett-Packard's $15 Million race toward social justice*. Stanford, CA: Stanford University Press.

Fetterman, D. M. (2013b). Empowerment evaluation: Learning to think like an evaluator. In M. Alkin (Ed.), *Evaluation roots: A wider perspective of theorists' views and influences* (2nd ed.). Thousand Oaks, CA: SAGE.

Fetterman, D. M. (2015a). Empowerment evaluation and action research: A convergence of values, principles, and purpose. In H. Bradbury (Ed.), *The SAGE handbook of action research*. Thousand Oaks, CA: SAGE.

Fetterman, D. M. (2015b). Empowerment evaluation and evaluation capacity building in a 10-year tobacco prevention initiative. In D. M. Fetterman, S. Kaftarian, & A. Wandersman (Eds.), *Empowerment evaluation: Knowledge and tools for self-assessment, evaluation capacity building, and accountability* (2nd ed.). Thousand Oaks, CA: SAGE.

Fetterman, D. M. (2015c). Empowerment evaluation: Theories, principles, concepts, and steps. In D. M. Fetterman, S. Kaftarian, & A. Wandersman (Eds.), *Empowerment evaluation: Knowledge and tools for self-assessment, evaluation capacity building, and accountability* (2nd ed.). Thousand Oaks, CA: SAGE.

Fetterman, D. M. (2017). Transformative empowerment evaluation and Freirean pedagogy: Alignment with an emancipatory tradition. *New Directions for Evaluation, 155*, 111–126.

Fetterman, D. M. (2018). A Google-enhanced empowerment evaluation approach in a graduate school program. In D. M. Fetterman, L. Rodríguez-Campos, A. P. Zukoski, & Contributors (Eds.), *Collaborative, participatory, and empowerment evaluation: Stakeholder involvement approaches.* New York: Guilford Press.

Fetterman, D. M. (2020). *Ethnography: Step by Step* (4th ed.). Thousand Oaks, CA: SAGE.

Fetterman, D. M. (2022). *Graduate addiction studies program 4th quarter evaluation report.* Hadley, MA: Fetterman & Associates.

Fetterman, D. M., & Bowman, C. (2002). Experiential education and empowerment evaluation: Mars rover educational program case example. *Journal of Experiential Education, 25*(2), 286–295.

Fetterman, D. M., Deitz, J., & Gesundheit, N. (2010). Empowerment evaluation: A collaborative approach to evaluating and transforming a medical school curriculum. *Academic Medicine, 85*(5), 813–820.

Fetterman, D. M., Delaney, L., Triana-Tremain, B., & Evans-Lee, M. (2015). Empowerment evaluation and evaluation capacity building in a 10-year tobacco prevention initiative. In D. M. Fetterman, S. Kaftarian, & A. Wandersman (Eds.), *Empowerment evaluation: Knowledge and tools for self-assessment, evaluation capacity building, and accountability* (2nd ed.). Thousand Oaks, CA: SAGE.

Fetterman, D. M., Kaftarian, S. J., & Wandersman, A. (Eds.). (1996). *Empowerment evaluation: Knowledge and tools for self-assessment and accountability.* Thousand Oaks, CA: SAGE.

Fetterman, D. M., Kaftarian, S., & Wandersman, A. (Eds.). (2015). *Empowerment evaluation: Knowledge and tools for self-assessment, evaluation capacity building, and accountability* (2nd ed.). Thousand Oaks, CA: SAGE.

Fetterman, D. M., Rodríguez-Campos, L., Zukoski, A. P., & Contributors. (2018). *Collaborative, participatory, and empowerment evaluation: Stakeholder involvement approaches.* New York: Guilford Press.

Fetterman, D. M., & Wandersman, A. (Eds.). (2005). *Empowerment evaluation principles in practice.* New York: Guilford Press.

Fetterman, D. M., & Wandersman, A. (2007). Empowerment evaluation: Yesterday, today, and tomorrow. *American Journal of Evaluation, 28*(2), 179–198.

Fetterman, D. M., & Wandersman, A. (2017). Celebrating the 21st anniversary of empowerment evaluation with our critical friends. *Evaluation and Program Planning, 63*, 132–135.

Field, A. (2017). *Discovering statistics using IBM SPSS Statistics: North American edition* (5th ed.). Thousand Oaks, CA: SAGE.

Foley, K. E., & Daniels, E. (2022, May 28). Proposed menthol ban divides Black leaders. Retrieved from *www.politico.com/news/2022/04/28/proposed-menthol-ban-divides-black-leaders-00028750.*

Freire, P. (1974). *Pedagogy of the oppressed.* New York: Seabury Press.

Freire, P. (1985). *The politics of education: Culture, power, and liberation.* Granby, MA: Bergin & Garvey.

Freire, P. (1997). *Pedagogia da Automomia: Saberes necessários à prática educativa.* São Paulo, Brazil: Paz e Terra.

Giovino, G. A., Villanti, A. C., Mowery, P. D., Sevilimedu, V., Niaura, R. S., Vallone, D. M., et al. (2015). Differential trends in cigarette smoking in the USA: Is menthol slowing progress? *Tobacco Control, 24*(1), 28–37.

Jackson, K., & Bazely, P. (2021). *Qualitative data analysis with NVivo.* Thousand Oaks, CA: SAGE.

Joint Committee on Standards for Educational Evaluation. (1994). *The program evaluation standards.* Thousand Oaks, CA: SAGE.

Kanem, N. (2022). *Seeing the unseen: The case for action in the neglected crisis of unintended pregnancy.* New York: United Nations Population Fund.

Kochanek, K. D., Murphy, S. L., Xu, J. Q., & Tejada-Vera, B. (2016). Deaths: Final data for 2014. *National Vital Statistics Reports, 65*(4), 1–122.

Labin, S. N., Duffy, J. L., Meyers, D. C., Wandersman, A., & Lesesne, C. A. (2013). A research synthesis of the evaluation capacity building literature. *American Journal of Evaluation, 33*(3), 307–308.

Langhout, R. D., & Fernandez, J. S. (2015). Empowerment evaluation conducted by fourth- and fifth-grade students. In D. M. Fetterman, S. Kaftarian, & A. Wandersman (Eds.), *Empowerment evaluation: Knowledge and tools for self-assessment, evaluation capacity building, and accountability* (2nd ed.). Thousand Oaks, CA: SAGE.

Lentz, B. E., Imm, P. S., Yost, J. B., Johnson, N. P., Barron, C., Lindberg, M. S., et al. (2005). Empowerment evaluation and organizational learning: A case study of a community coalition designed to prevent child abuse and neglect. In D. M. Fetterman & A. Wandersman (Eds.), *Empowerment evaluation principles in practice.* New York: Guilford Press.

Modi, N. (2018, March 13). Address by Prime Minister Narendra Modi. Presented at the *Delhi End TB Summit.*

Patton, M. Q. (1997a). Toward distinguishing empowerment evaluation and placing it in a larger context. *Evaluation Practice, 18*(2)147–163.

Patton, M. Q. (1997b). *Utilization-focused evaluation.* Thousand Oaks, CA: SAGE.

Patton, M. Q. (2005). Toward distinguishing empowerment evaluation and placing it in a larger context; take two. *American Journal of Evaluation, 26,* 408–414.

Patton, M. Q. (2015). [Review of the book *Empowerment evaluation: Knowledge and tools for self-assessment, evaluation capacity building, and accountability* (2nd ed.)]. *Evaluation and Program Planning, 52,* 15–18

Patton, M. Q. (2017). Empowerment evaluation: Exemplary in its openness to dialogue, reflective practice, and process use. *Evaluation and Program Planning, 63,* 139–140.

Perkins, D., & Zimmerman, M. (1995). Empowerment theory, research, and application. *American Journal of Community Psychology, 23*(5), 569–579.

Ramanathan, N., Fruchterman, J., Fowler, A., & Carotti-Sha, G. (2022). Decolonize data. *Stanford Social Innovation Review, 20*(2), 59–60.

Romans, A., Stancieland, C., & Harley, T. (2022, May 24). Measuring is an act of power: A call for pro-Black measurement and evaluation. Retrieved from *https://nonprofitquarterly.org/measuring-is-an-act-of-power-a-call-for-pro-black-measurement-and-evaluation.* (Originally published in Going pro-Black: What would a pro-Black sector sound, look, taste, and feel like? *Nonprofit Quarterly*, Spring 2022, 94–100.)

Roth, C. (2022). Unplanned pregnancy is a "crisis." Deutsche Welle. Available online at *https://www.dw.com/en/unplanned-pregnancy-is-a-crisis-all-around-us/a-61314434.*

Sachdeva, K. S. (2020). Accelerating progress toward ending tuberculosis in India. *Indian Journal of Medical Research, 151*(4), 266–268.

Saldana, J. (2021). *The Coding manual for qualitative researchers* (4th ed.). Thousand Oaks, CA: SAGE.

Salkind, N. J., & Frey, B. B. (2019). *Statistics for people who (think they) hate statistics* (7th ed.). Thousand Oaks, CA: SAGE.

Sastre-Merino, S. Vidueira, P., Díaz-Puente, J., & Fernández-Moral, M. J. (2015). Capacity building through empowerment evaluation: An Aymara women artisans organization in Puno, Peru. In D. M. Fetterman, S. Kaftarian, & A. Wandersman (Eds.), *Empowerment evaluation: Knowledge and tools for self-assessment, evaluation capacity building, and accountability* (2nd ed.). Thousand Oaks, CA: SAGE.

Schoenborn, C. A., Adams, P. F., & Peregoy, J. A. (2013). *Health behaviors of adults: United States, 2008–2010 [PDF - 3.2MB].* National Center for Health Statistics. Vital Health Stat 10(257),

Scriven, M. (1997). Empowerment evaluation examined. *Evaluation Practice, 18*(2), 165–175.

Scriven, M. (2017). Empowerment evaluation 21 years later: There is much to admire about empowerment evaluation. *Evaluation and Program Planning, 63*, 138.

Sechrest, L. (1997). [Review of the book *Empowerment evaluation: Knowledge and tools for self-assessment and accountability* by D. M. Fetterman, S. J. Kaftarian, & A. Wandersman (Eds.]. *Environment and Behavior, 29*(3), 422–426.

Sharma, N. C. (2018, March 14). India aims to eliminate tuberculosis by 2025: Narendra Modi. Retrieved from *www.livemint.com/Politics/a3hJk9SqqilPZUtO0vAHN/PM-Modi-launches-campaign-to-eradicate-TB-from-India-by-2025.html.*

Shaull, R. (1974). Foreword. In P. Freire, *Pedagogy of the oppressed.* New York: Seabury Press.

Smith, C. (personal communication, 2004).

Stufflebeam, D. L. (1994). Empowerment evaluation, objectivist evaluation, and evaluation standards: Where the future of evaluation should not go and where it needs to go. *Evaluation Practice, 15*(3), 321–228.

Taylor-Ritzler, T., Suarez-Balcazar, Y., Garcia-Iriarte, E., Henry, D., & Balcazar, F. (2013). Understanding and measuring evaluation capacity: A model and instrument validation study. *American Journal of Evaluation, 34*, 190–206.

U.S. Department of Health and Human Services. (1998). *Tobacco use among U.S. racial/ethnic minority groups—African Americans, American Indians and Alaska Natives, Asian Americans and Pacific Islanders, and Hispanics: A report of the Surgeon General.* Atlanta, GA: U.S. Department of Health and Human Services, Centers for Disease Control and Prevention, Office on Smoking and Health.

U.S. Department of Health and Human Services. (2014). *The health consequences of smoking—50 years of progress: A report of the Surgeon General.* Atlanta, GA: U.S. Department of Health and Human Services, Centers for Disease Control and Prevention, National Center for Chronic Disease Prevention and Health Promotion, Office on Smoking and Health.

Villanti, A. C., Johnson A. L, Ambrose, B. K., Cummings, K. M., Stanton, C. A., Rose, S. W., et al. (2017). Flavored tobacco product use in youth and adults: Findings from the first wave of the PATH study (2013–2014). *American Journal of Preventive Medicine, 53*(2), 139–151.

Wandersman, A., Keener, D. C., Snell-Johns, J., Miller, R., Flaspohler, P., Dye, M., et al. (2004). Empowerment evaluation: Principles in action. In L. A. Jason, C. B. Keys, Y. Suarez-Balcazar, R. R. Taylor, M. Davis, J. Durlak, et al. (Eds.), *Participatory community research: Theories and methods in action.* Washington, DC: American Psychological Association.

Wandersman, A., Snell-Johns, J., Lentz, B., Fetterman, D. M., Keener, D. C., Livet, M., et al. (2005). The principles of empowerment evaluation. In D. M. Fetterman & A. Wandersman (Eds.), *Empowerment evaluation principles in practice.* New York: Guilford Press.

Wild, T. (1997). [Review of the book *Empowerment evaluation: Knowledge and tools for self-assessment and accountability* by D. M. Fetterman, S. J. Kaftarian, & A. Wandersman (Eds.)]. *Canadian Journal of Program Evaluation, 11*(2), 170–172.

Wilson, R. (personal communication, 2004).

Worthen, B. (personal communication, 1997).

World Health Organization. (2008). *Report on the global tobacco epidemic, 2008: The MPOWER package.* Geneva, Switzerland: Author.

World Health Organization. (2021). *Tuberculosis.* Geneva, Switzerland: Author.

Zimmerman, M. (2000). Empowerment theory. In J. Rappaport & E. Seidman (Eds.), *Handbook of community psychology.* New York: Kluwer Academic/Plenum.

Index

About the Author

David M. Fetterman, PhD, is president and CEO of Fetterman and Associates, an international evaluation consulting firm, and the founder of empowerment evaluation. Dr. Fetterman has worked in more than 17 countries—in South African townships and Native American reservations, as well as in Silicon Valley tech firms, including Google and Hewlett-Packard—and has 25 years of experience at Stanford University, serving as a School of Education faculty member, the School of Medicine director of evaluation, and a senior member of the University administration. He currently serves as a faculty member at Pacifica Graduate Institute and Claremont Graduate University. Dr. Fetterman is past president of the American Evaluation Association (AEA) and the Council on Anthropology and Education of the American Anthropological Association (AAA). He is a recipient of honors including the Paul F. Lazarsfeld Evaluation Theory Award and the Alva and Gunnar Myrdal Evaluation Practice Award from the AEA; the President's Award from the AAA; the Distinguished Scholar Award from the Research on Evaluation Special Interest Group of the American Educational Research Association; and the Award for Excellence in Research from the Mensa Foundation. He is the author or editor of numerous books.